PRAISE FOR

Overmedicated and Undertreated:
How I Lost My Only Son to Today's Toxic Children's Mental Health Industry

"This is an important book, wonderfully done. Steven Francesco brings a unique and valuable hybrid perspective to the topic. He weaves a story with a powerful message for all involved in today's U.S. children's mental health world. His recommendations are well thought-out and merit serious consideration by parents and mental health professionals."

— **Elisabeth Rosenthal,** Senior Writer, *New York Times*
Recipient of the 2014 Victor Cohn Prize for Excellence in Medical Science Reporting

"*Overmedicated and Undertreated* is absorbing and deeply saddening. Steven Francesco's writing vividly captures the tragic consequences of an overly medicalized approach to treating young people with psychiatric problems and highlights the urgency of moving the mental health care of our children and adolescents in a new direction."

— **Mark Olfson, MD,** Professor of Psychiatry, Columbia University Medical Center

OVERMEDICATED
&UNDERTREATED

How I Lost My Only Son to Today's
Toxic Children's Mental Health Industry

STEVEN FRANCESCO

Dedication

To the many thousands of caregivers, parents, family members and others who have responsibility for our emotionally disturbed children. Each day you have a difficult, frustrating and largely thankless task. You and the many wonderful mental health professionals with whom you have contact are doing your best.

However, helping our challenged children is getting more difficult each day due to the many distortions and hidden influences within the current toxic children's mental health industry.

I hope *Overmedicated and Undertreated* provides enlightenment. It is intended to contain valuable insight and guidance, provide some measure of relief and help you anticipate future problems as you and your children cope with your ever-changing challenges.

Finally, perhaps working together, we may trigger reform for a children's mental health industry that has lost its way. From psychiatrists to insurance and drug companies to schools, few of them are working together to give our children the focused care they really need.

Contents

INTRODUCTION

January 2015

In the winter of 2009, my fifteen-year-old son, Andrew, died from an adverse reaction to a popularly prescribed psychiatric drug. He was fine on a Friday night, in a vegetative state on Sunday morning, and never emerged.

Andrew was a lively, funny, and extraordinarily athletic child. Although he struggled with mental health problems—as well as frequent, destabilizing school reassignments—for most of his young life, I had high hopes for his future. He received many diagnoses over the years, including obsessive-compulsive disorder, Tourette's syndrome, bipolar disorder, and ADHD, for which he was prescribed a varied and rotating menu of potent medications.

I loved my son and miss him every day. Andrew's struggle with mental illness lacked a proven course of treatment or tidy summa-

ry, as anyone with direct experience of mental illness will understand. And, like most parents with a child in crisis, I relied heavily
on the expertise and advice of medical professionals, school of-
ficials, and other authority figures. Andrew, in fact, was luckier
than many children in this country. He had parents who could
access the very best resources for care. Yet, in the end, that made
no difference—we lost him.

Though I felt that I did everything possible to help him
overcome his mental health condition, I can't help but still ask
myself: what could I have done differently? I never suspected
at the time that despite the apparent good intentions of those
who tried to help him, there were larger trends at play that put
my son in jeopardy. Perhaps I should have. After a thirty-year career in health care—nine years as senior management of marketing and strategy for several drug manufacturers and twenty-one
years subsequently running my own independent health care
consultancy—I thought I knew the health care industry as well
as anyone.

Until Andrew's first diagnosis, however, I sat at a safe distance
from some damaging ground-level effects of the business. When
Andrew was at risk, I was painfully unaware of the serious issue
of inappropriate and systematized overprescribing of powerful
drugs to children—drugs that in most cases were designed and
approved for adults only. I was unaware that insurance companies discouraged therapeutic alternatives to drugs, unaware of the
tremendous pressure from schools to medicate children, and unaware that drug companies had been repeatedly fined for illegally
promoting that doctors prescribe drugs to children without evidence of efficacy, safety, or FDA approval.

Before Andrew died, I'd never even heard of neuroleptic malignant syndrome (NMS), a known and sudden side effect caused

by taking excessively large doses of atypical antipsychotic drugs over long periods of time.[1] Andrew's doctors never raised the possibility of this condition with us. Looking back, I only wish that I had had a place to go, a resource for guidance and support, for the shared experience of someone who'd already been through the process.

Caring for a child with mental health difficulties can feel extremely stressful and isolating. For millions of American families currently caught in the web of what I call today's toxic children's mental health industry, I intend this book to alert, educate, and provide comfort and commiseration in difficult and emotional situations. As caregivers, we are called upon to deploy a wide range of skills. We must take care of our children as best we can every day, and we must know how to manage for our families within the system. It is no easy task.

This book explores my son Andrew's child psychiatric experience and what it was like for those close to him. I hope that sharing these experiences can help others steer clear of or better navigate the many specific challenges that confronted us. I hope that others may learn from both our successes and our failures. For more day-to-day support and discussion, kindly go to my new website, DoNoHarmNetwork.Org

The Notes section at the end of the book offers additional sources of discussion on key points and useful information, including the evidence behind some assertions in the narrative. There's also an abundance of medical/research information not usually available to the consumer. A chapter-by-chapter Reading Guide of questions and comments to further assist the reader on this important subject, as well as additional valuable information, is available at the website for this book, OvermedicatedandUndertreated.com.

It is worth noting: All names have been changed with the exception of mine and my son. Also, all data—dates, drugs and dosages as well as events are factual, drawn from actual documents that were used in the malpractice case filed after Andrew's death as well as our own family computer files.

Writing this book was an equally painful and therapeutic experience for me, and I sincerely hope that by sharing an intensely personal story, I can help others successfully deal with our byzantine and dangerously drug-oriented children's mental health industry. I believe we as a nation deserve a better system. I know my son did.

PROLOGUE

Sunday, January 18, 2008, 7:30 AM

"Andrew, let them put on the oxygen mask. Let them put it on," I plead, crouched in the back of an ambulance.

The ambulance is racing to the emergency room of St. Barnabas Hospital in Livingston, New Jersey. There are the deep voices of other men in the ambulance, trying to get my son to accept the mask. He is resisting every effort to place a mask over his nose, as if it contains a poison.

"Andrew, listen to me. Let them put the mask on. They want to help."

I'm doing everything in my power to stay calm and reassure him, to stem his panic. The medics have strapped fifteen-year-old Andrew to the gurney, but he is still able to get his arms free and resist the mask. He is suffering terribly, barely able to breathe yet fighting against any help. I watch his skin change

5

from olive to ghastly pale blue. He needs oxygen immediately.

I'm talking loudly now over the sound of the ambulance. I hope the sound of my voice can bring him relief, something to cut through his panic and assure him that the strange faces and commotion around him are here to help.

"Andrew . . . Listen to me! Andrew! Andrew!" I keep repeating, hoping to get through. But it is pointless. He is already in another space, past any reason and utterly alone. I feel helpless and sick watching Andrew, blank-eyed, gasp and flail atop the gurney. I am unable to bring any relief to my beloved son.

Tragically, no one could.

CHAPTER ONE

The Beginning

Pediatric Neurology in Livingston, NJ
December 11, 1996

Andrew's introduction to "the system"—so to speak—came early, at the age of three. My wife Mary and I sat in the office of Dr. Johnson, a specialist in pediatric neurology, as Andrew patrolled the carpet around our feet.

About six months earlier, in the back seat of our car returning from a family beach trip, Andrew had started babbling in his car seat. His older sister Margaux, sitting beside him, at first wasn't sure whether to laugh or to be frightened. For almost ten minutes it was as if he'd left his body, making incoherent sounds with his eyes rolled up into the back of his head. It was terrifying, and, despite our increasingly desperate efforts to stop or interrupt him, he kept on. We pulled to the side of the highway and spoke to him. We grasped and shook his tiny hands—anything we could do to coax him out of his state, to no avail. Eventually his eyes dropped back into place and he looked at us, confused by the attention, but fine, like nothing had happened. We drove home on high alert, but the episode never repeated.

It was about three months later, in July, that Andrew began a pattern of similarly distressing behavior. While sitting in his high chair eating, he would begin to bob his head back and forth, again with his eyes rolling back, like his spirit had escaped to another place. After a minute or so, he would return to normal and continue to eat, as if time had simply paused for him. The episodes were happening frequently, and we took him to see our pediatrician. The pediatrician referred us to Dr. Johnson.

Mary and I sat across the desk. We nervously hoped for an answer, or at least some variety of comfort or recognition from this expert.

"The three-minute EEG test was impossible to complete," he began with noticeable irritation. "Andrew kept pulling off the electrodes."

Andrew was a handful, it was true. From his first baby steps, he was on the go, exploring, moving around, and discovering the world around him. Though I suspected that sitting still with wires attached to the head was a lot to ask from any three-year-old.

"Some kids accept them, and others don't," Dr. Johnson continued. "So, here's where we are. The babbling and the head-bobbing could suggest epilepsy, but there are other potential diagnoses as well. It's hard to tell with what little information we have. I'd like to have some more comprehensive testing, including a twenty-four-hour electroencephalogram."

It was obvious from his tone that this test wasn't designed for children either. Mary and I just looked at one another, then at Andrew motoring around the floor of the office. Both at a loss, we waited expectantly for what he would say next.

"It's possible also that there may be nothing going on neurologically, and that the episodes are just part of a developmental stage your son is going through."

Hearing the expert even suggest that Andrew's episodes were nothing more than a passing phase brought me the first calm moment that I'd felt in a while.

"So, we have three options to consider," he went on. "One, we could simply continue to monitor Andrew's behavior. We would want to look for more frequent episodes, or longer ones, or anything new that you feel is unusual—a wait-and-see approach. Children do develop quickly and go through stages. Your son might simply outgrow this behavior.

"The second option involves a twenty-four-hour ambulatory EEG to discover whether there are areas of his brain that are not functioning correctly because of either too little or too much electrical activity. The test can identify mild brain seizures," he went on dispassionately. "The EEG is usually done at home and is recorded on a small computer disk worn in a case around the patient's waist. It would require attaching small electrodes to the scalp with a special skin glue. The data on the disk is then uploaded to a computer where it can be read and interpreted by a neurologist."

I doubted strongly that the glue would be toddler-proof, and by Mary's expression she seemed to agree with me.

"The third option is to give him a medication, probably Depakote, that we use to treat epilepsy. If the episodes of head-bobbing and babbling stop, then we would assume that he is epileptic and continue to monitor and medicate him."

I was staring at Dr. Johnson, but noticed that Andrew had

stopped moving around the floor. He studied the weave of the carpeting. It's difficult to imagine what a three-year-old might experience during a doctor visit like this, but I suspected that he sensed the fear and confusion Mary and I were doing our best to hide.

As Mary and I listened to Dr. Johnson, a top expert, speak, it seemed that an explanation for Andrew's condition was only moving further out of reach. As a longtime professional in the field of health care, deeply familiar with the workings of the industry, I found this confusion doubly frustrating. Why couldn't we work together and get a straight answer?

Mary looked at me expectantly, but I was ill-equipped to bring any more clarity to the situation. Dr. Johnson had four years of medical school, a minimum two years of pediatric residency, and three additional years of residency training in neurology—yet he was deflecting a choice of action back to us. Dr. Spock's *Baby and Child Care* did not prepare us for anything like this. And, in 1996, the Internet had nothing to add.

Sometimes as a parent you are faced with decisions involving your children that are very difficult to sort out, ones that come without any blueprint or even anecdotal guidance. This one was our first with Andrew.

Giving Andrew epilepsy drugs without even a diagnosis seemed backward and irresponsible to me. Introducing potent chemicals into the system of a defenseless and unaware child, to medicate him for a condition that we didn't even know he actually had, made me deeply uncomfortable. The idea felt like turning my son into a laboratory experiment. However, the doctor appeared perfectly cavalier toward the approach. I was overwhelmed and shocked, left to wonder: was this the state of the art in children's health?

In that dizzying moment, I also lacked the presence of mind to ask Dr. Johnson a series of critical questions. *How soon would we quit dosing Andrew if we saw no change? If the condition turned out to be developmental and Andrew's behavior came around, how would we know it wasn't attributable to the medication? What side effects were possible from this medication, especially side effects specific to a small child with an evolving brain?*

Mary and I decided to leave and consider our options before taking any further steps. We stopped off at the Livingston Mall on the drive home to let Andrew wander around and burn some energy. Mary let him pick out a treat as a reward for his composure during the stressful visit to the doctor, and while she took him off shopping, I sought refuge in Barnes and Noble. Leaving Dr. Johnson's office, I had pressed his staff for a copy of the dictated report from our visit. It turned out to be a surprisingly difficult process, but I waited and finally received it. The report initially repeated what we had communicated in our meeting with the doctor, but the additional information in medical language struck me. It described some issues that were not mentioned to us, his parents:

Perhaps up to a dozen times a day, and it occurs daily, he'll bob his head, have a blank look, his eyes will roll up. It lasts one or two seconds. There is no regularity to it. There has been no change in frequency or duration. There is no other change in tone, no temporary lethargic state that occurs after a seizure. There is no loss of consciousness, muscle stiffness or jerky activity. This has been confirmed by his parents and the babysitter. No family history of seizures, epilepsy or other neurological disorders.

Assessment: The history is suggestive of absence seizure activity. The differential may include behavioral changes. However, with no sudden dramatic change of activity or physical movement the nature of the event of that is less likely. As there is no major change in tone or change in color, a sudden change in heartbeat or patterned irregular heartbeat is unlikely. Metabolic causes are unlikely, given the episodic nature.

At Barnes and Noble I searched for books on medicine, specifically pediatric neurology. I didn't expect to find many medical texts in a consumer chain bookstore, but the phrase "absence seizure activity"[1] had lodged in my brain. Though admittedly my mind was swimming during the meeting, I didn't recall Dr. Johnson mentioning it to us. I was looking for any information, hoping to move closer to some answer for Andrew.

I found a shelf of medical books and went diving through the indexes. Though I couldn't find any mention of absence seizure activity, I did take some comfort from just being in the bookstore—a bright space full of books and ideas—as I struggled to process my thoughts.

When Mary and Andrew found me in the Barnes and Noble, Andrew was jumping with excitement to show me a new red Pez dispenser, filled with a fresh column of candy. He was behaving like his usual adorable self, but I couldn't fully enjoy the moment. I remember that Mary and I didn't talk much on the drive home. I was deep in thought, and I assume that she was as well.

The route home from the mall took us down South Orange Avenue, one of the longest streets in New Jersey. It cuts through many cities and is also known as the Columbia Turnpike or Route 510. It runs thirty miles from the heart of Newark all the way to Morristown, and there are twisty, hilly stretches and long straightaways. All along it are parks, schools, churches, malls, condominiums, and houses that advertise an affluent and hopeful microcosm of a prosperous nation. On this drive, however, my eyes continually fell on signage for doctors' offices, pharmacies, and drugstores—the catchy, bright lettering for CVS and Duane Reade. I noticed for the first time how some of these drug outlet storefronts were actually converted bank buildings, with grand columns outside to greet customers. Passing by them, I wondered if there was a cure for Andrew tucked away inside their aisles, if they were a place where we could place our trust.

As I pulled into our driveway and we all took a breath amid the familiar shapes, colors, and textures of home, it became clear what Mary and I would decide. Without speaking, we both knew that we would take the wait-and-see approach Dr. Johnson had offered as the second option. It was the most viable approach, considering Andrew's high activity level, and we could both sleep knowing we were not doing anything that could affect the developing brain chemistry of a small child. This hands-off approach did require some faith, but in lieu of conclusive results or useful medical advice, faith was all we could lean on.

CHAPTER TWO

Different Sides Emerge

September–November 1998

Our faith turned out to be well placed. Around three months after the visit to Dr. Johnson, Andrew's head bobbing disappeared, and the Francesco family pressed ahead. Young Andrew continued to bound through life with outsized energy and uncanny coordination. His activity level did not diminish: in fact, it only seemed to increase along with his body size.

He began preschool and managed to stand out even among four-year-olds for being rambunctious and difficult to herd back into the classroom after outside time. I can remember the preschool director giving me weary smiles of commiseration when

Andrew tore out from the line to meet me at pickup time. At home, he loved to be around any action. Andrew mimicked Mary cooking in the kitchen and loved to dig weeds beside me outside our house. We began to see some early hints of Andrew's trouble relating to other kids around this time, but his bright, outsized spirit and energy gave us reassurance.

Andrew more or less crash-landed into kindergarten. His teacher Mrs. Campbell provided us with regular reports of a loving energy bundle who often made her job difficult in creative ways. When the other kids sat down to work on pictures, Andrew wanted to build towers with the paint bottles. He had trouble staying on task. He constantly looked for ways to get up and move around. He would ask to go to the water fountain during his classmates' presentations. He would climb under the tables during lessons.

Andrew's sister Margaux had glided through her entry into school. She had handled it much more gracefully, in fact, than her nervous and excited parents. About the only feedback we got for Margaux was quiet approval or outright praise. With Andrew, we quickly noticed a new pattern of extra conversations and sideways expressions from his teachers and administrators. Mary and I were unsure how much of Andrew's behavior to attribute to basic personality differences or to basic little-boy chemistry.

Andrew's kindergarten eventually suggested that we have Andrew evaluated by a child psychiatrist. Mary and I immediately agreed and scheduled the appointment. We welcomed the advice of an outside expert, having no blueprint to raise a little boy whose energy was increasingly difficult to corral into social settings. With things moving at life-speed, it can be hard to stop and consider the wider and future implications of such choices. It's often impossible to recognize the first innocent step down a path that leads quickly into deeper forest. We, of course, well remembered his earlier spells, but didn't see any potential correlation with Andrew's overly kinetic urges at school.

Rather than an open and sympathetic engagement with Andrew as the patient, though, our visits to the child psychiatrist felt more like driving through a fast-food restaurant. Dr. Pinketty's office was painted in warm bright colors, and the waiting room was stocked with toys. He asked a series of scripted questions about Andrew's behavior at school. I'd met many doctors in my line of work, and I believed that Dr. Pinketty had only Andrew's best interests in mind, but still, I couldn't shake the feeling of being shuffled through a production line. The doctor seemed relatively unconcerned with Andrew's past or the particular conditions of his acting out.

After just three sessions with Dr. Pinketty, Andrew was diagnosed with attention deficit hyperactivity disorder (ADHD) and mild oppositional tendencies. He was prescribed 2.5 milligrams of Ritalin twice a day. I challenged Dr. Pinketty on his ADHD diagnosis directly, arguing that Andrew was simply being a young boy. Over 80% of Ritalin prescriptions go to boys.

"Mr. Francesco, that is my diagnosis," he replied coolly. "I am the doctor here."

Mary and I felt quite alone and helpless as parents. Many of our questions fell flat. *Could Andrew potentially grow out of his restlessness, as he had his head-bobbing? How long was Andrew likely to stay on the medication?* No relevant data was available from the doctor. I wished for an outside coach or mentor to talk with, another parent who had come through the process already. The still-new Internet also failed to provide any reassuring narrative around the drug approach. Talking with friends and neighbors provided us little relief. Mary and I came to learn of other kids in our community, as young as three years old, who were being given

Ritalin or similar drugs for ADHD,[1] but I found the notion very hard to accept for five-year-old Andrew.

After more argument, Dr. Pinketty reluctantly offered six family counseling sessions, in addition to Andrew's required "medication management" appointments, to assuage me. Ritalin is not FDA-approved for children under six years old, but a widely used principle known as medication management makes it possible for doctors to issue a prescription anyway. Medication management is based on the understanding that drugs that are FDA-approved for different conditions or different populations may also hold other benefits. In Andrew's case, Ritalin was FDA-approved to treat ADHD in older children, so it was assumed that the drug might also be effective for Andrew. The principle of medication management allows doctors to prescribe outside the confines of FDA approval, so long as they closely and continuously monitor the patient.

Mary and I had hoped to leave Dr. Pinketty's office with useful new parenting tools or information, rather than a lonely slip from his prescription pad. As we drove down South Orange Avenue, I felt a familiar discomfort over feeding powerful chemicals to my young son without convincing data or a template for his potential improvement. We couldn't deny, however, that Andrew's behavior at school was troubling. He had not been able to relate to his peers as easily as Margaux had. Lots of evidence showed that he was far more comfortable on the playground than he was in the classroom. It was a situation that clearly couldn't continue indefinitely. We weren't shocked by the outcome with Dr. Pinketty, but we were unprepared.

Mary and I watched Andrew barrel out of the car and directly over to the basket of sports equipment in our garage. It was still light out, and he went to play soccer in the yard. He needed to move around after being cooped up in Dr. Pinketty's office. Mary and I shut the garage door and stayed in the car to discuss what we should do.

"I don't like it either," she said. "Giving him drugs just to sit still . . . it feels wrong."

The school was indirectly pressuring us to medicate. We'd agreed to report back immediately with the advice from Dr. Pinketty. It felt like sides lining up against us in a battle. Though Mrs. Campbell and the principal, Mr. Everett, presented their suggestion to have Andrew seen with a tone of support and concern, the subtext was clear: medicate him. For a busy educator, I can see how this is a relatively simple conclusion—one with growing precedent and traction. In the churn of daily school life, it boils down to simple arithmetic: given A (a child who can't focus), add B (pills) to get C (a more orderly classroom). Still, I was ready to fight.

"What else can we do?" Mary asked.

"We can refuse," I said.

"But what if things don't get any better?"

"Do you think we're there yet?" I wondered.

"Not yet . . . but I'm worried we're headed there."

"So we have time to wait and see."

We talked on in the car.

There was hope that things would turn around. Andrew had come through his head-bobbing just a few years before without chemical intervention. We reminisced about growing up in a different time, before it seemed common to medicate kids for minor misbehaviors. There was so much joy and spirit spilling from his little but growing body that, even assuming the best possible outcome, I couldn't bring myself to feel right about smothering or sedating it.

"Well. We're his parents, after all," Mary said.

We discussed whether we might be leading Andrew to problems in the future by potentially causing friction with the school. But Mary's simple statement seemed to snap our thinking into place. It was dusk outside and nearly dark inside the garage. We'd turned on the ignition lights, but needed to get inside and put on dinner.

I wished I could have left Dr. Pinketty's prescription in a drawer and thought about whether I should fill it; however, the school pressure was too great. We started giving Andrew Ritalin at six years old.

CHAPTER THREE

The FDA Meeting

May 10–11, 2001

"Hey, Dad," eight-year-old Andrew called from outside my home office. I was hunched over my desk preparing remarks for a major FDA conference the next day, palms sweaty. I turned toward Andrew's voice, but he was not there. Angry at being disturbed, I swiveled my chair fully around; still, no Andrew.

"Hey, Dad," he said again, smiling down at me from the ceiling.

Andrew had shimmied up the doorframe and managed to wedge his little body there at the top like Spider-Man.

"How'd you get up there?" I asked.

"I took the elevator," he said, still smiling proudly.

I was unable to properly enjoy this moment, my head swimming as it was with thoughts and anxieties for the day to come. "Very impressive," I said. I'd never seen this trick of his before. "I still have some work to finish up, though. OK, Big Guy? I'll come join everybody in the living room in a few minutes."

"Sure, Dad," Andrew said. He dropped to the floor, landing gracefully, and disappeared around the corner.

At the FDA conference, I was scheduled to face off against several former colleagues. The professional risk for me was potentially huge. This conference in Rockville, MD, was the most public, high-level speaking appearance of my career. At fifty-one years old, with a loving wife and two beautiful children, I was starting to wonder: was it even worth it?

The FDA conference was to argue an unprecedented Citizen's Petition by Wellpoint Insurance of California to reclassify a group of non-sedating antihistamine drugs (on which I was an expert) from prescription to over-the-counter legal status (OTC). By moving these medications to OTC status in the U.S., insurance companies could instantly add several hundred million dollars to their collective bottom line because they would no longer reimburse for them—a huge savings. As a respected independent consultant to pharmaceutical companies, specializing in market analysis and public health potential for precisely this type of drug reclassification, I knew the topic as well as anyone in the world.

Beyond any point of professional pride, or any calculated business risk, I felt that I needed to be there. Speaking out against my former colleagues had the potential to be either highly destructive or highly beneficial for my new company. But there was something deeper, something more personal, gnawing at me.

Andrew's medication regimen had expanded and evolved. He

had moved from Ritalin to Concerta and then to back to Ritalin with Catapres to help him sleep at night. The school was adamant that his behavior had to change in class. Medication was seen as the solution, yet again.

My nerves were jangling over tomorrow's confrontation. Exhilaration for the professional honor, anxiety over potential alienation from my former colleagues, many of whom I considered friends, and simple adrenalin for the impending fight—all were traffic jammed in my psyche. And deeper still in my chest was a rising ethical doubt and distaste over Andrew's new treatment. I was making a good living from the pharmaceutical industry, but thinking about my young son forced onto behavior medication cracked something open in me. It went against all my instincts.

Our for-profit health care system is unique in the world. Directing multi-million-dollar pharmaceutical marketing initiatives in Europe and Asia, I'd come to learn many of the differences firsthand. These differences comprise very basic legal and political policy—but also, more subtly, differences in public expectations and differences of business culture inside the industry. Generally speaking, outside the U.S., health care is considered to be incompatible with standard free-market practice. In most other modern countries, basic health care is funded by taxes and operated by the government as a not-for-profit system. Its goal is to offer the best outcomes for the patients. Health care is considered a right of citizenship.

The foundational belief behind the U.S. system is that profit incentives drive innovation and health care progress—that our system ultimately provides superior care thanks to the incentives of the "invisible hand" of the market. Within this system, however, there can arise severe conflicts of interest, which are theoretically regulated by government bodies like the FDA. In Rockville,

I knew I was stepping into the middle of a battlefield. The two sides, insurers and drug makers, had enormous sums of money on the line in the fight over reclassification of these non-sedating antihistamine drugs. The rhetoric would center on public health and best outcomes for patients, but I knew intimately that the driving force behind each side was profit.

The manufacturers of non-sedating antihistamines (drugs like Claritin, Allegra, and Zyrtec) wanted to protect their prescription market—a cash cow for them worth around $3 billion in sales annually. Switching to OTC would drive down the prices substantially and shift the source of revenue from guaranteed lucrative reimbursement by insurers to erratic and fickle consumers in an openly competitive market.

Anyone in the health care field is unfortunately familiar with emotional, moral, ethical, and legal discomfort. I had started my own consulting firm in part to avoid such compromises. I loved my specialty (converting prescription drugs to OTC status, also called an Rx-to-OTC switch effort) without compunction because the work was geared toward the pragmatic improvement of public health.

Highly motivated representatives of companies like my last employer, Schering-Plough, were ready and waiting to "guide" the panel in Rockville toward an outcome in their financial favor. This was their job. I'd seen it done many times before. I felt extremely lucky to be speaking at the conference free from the political, dutiful pull toward ethical compromise one can feel inside a company. When one's livelihood is on the line, it is much easier to shift the ethical lens. I knew that a host of good soldiers would appear before the FDA doctor panel armed with misinformation and fearmongering presentations. They would not be happy to see me, nor to hear what I had to say.

Looking over my remarks that evening, though, I could barely muster proper concentration. Something else was worming around in the back of my mind. To me the conference was unnecessary, given the deep data and track record of non-sedating antihistamines. I wished instead for an equally energetic and well-funded public discussion of psychotropic medications and children's mental health. I wished I could step into a grand FDA debate over the treatment of seven-year-old boys with potent medications just for being active. As it was, I could only sit alone in my office, feeling at the mercy of larger, obscure forces.

I remembered taking a prescription stimulant similar to Ritalin one night while I was in college. There was an essay due the next day, and I needed to stay up all night to finish it. I cruised through to dawn, but crashed hard when the drug wore off. I thought the paper I turned in was great. Getting it back, however, I was surprised to discover that it was below average at best, full of incomplete and poorly thought-out ideas. Was this a potential mental effect that I was willing to foist on my young child?

Methylphenidate, the active ingredient of Ritalin, was approved for children's use by the FDA. But I also happened to know that its type of stimulant was prescribed to children in other countries on a drastically smaller scale. It seemed in other societies they were more willing to "let boys be boys." Why was my Andrew being drugged? Why was I allowing it? Was there another way to treat his restlessness without medication? What of old-fashioned patience by the teachers, helping him develop coping skills, or other such alternative therapies? What about better teacher training, or just plain old toleration? Or was my personal experience growing up perhaps playing too loudly in my mind? When I was five, I was kicked out of kindergarten on my second day. I refused to leave the sandbox after recess ended. My teacher told my parents I wasn't ready for school yet, but, over time, I learned to behave well enough in class. I still had occasional bouts of impulsivity throughout grade school, but that was what being a little boy in 1956 seemed to warrant. No one ever tried to drug me.

I decided to join my family in the living room to clear my head. Mary and Margaux were on one side of the sofa watching television, and Andrew was slumped on the other. I sat down next to Andrew and stroked his hair while he nodded out. In the calm of the moment, I tried to keep my mind open and accept that times change, that his treatment was state-of-the-art—that this was the height of collaborative wisdom from the best doctors and professional educators.

In Rockville my nerves came roaring back. The conference began with a statement by the FDA advisory committee chairman, and I got caught up in the excitement of a showdown. Despite the questionable motives of some participants, the conference itself was a noble and enlightened initiative. To gather such a highly educated and widely experienced group of experts, for the goal of advancing medical policy and public health, actually brought back a forgotten pride that I felt for the industry.

Government health boards are known to be highly cautious over the relaxing of control for prescription medications. However, American public health has clearly benefited from the wider OTC availability of former prescription-only treatments for headache, heartburn, arthritis pain, athlete's foot, coughs, colds, and so on. From my years of experience in foreign markets, I believed strongly that non-sedating antihistamines should be made available widely and without a prescription. They are safe and effective to treat highly common allergies such as hay fever. I knew from my work that these drugs were ready for reclassification, and that the FDA panel of doctors could not reasonably be shown any different. If the class of drugs carried any danger at all to public health, I would know about it.

I felt centered by this certainty, confident and ready. As a scheduled speaker, I was seated toward the front of the room. I settled into the hotel banquet-room chair to hear the presentations begin. Wellpoint presented first, and their PowerPoint mega-analysis was filled with scientific studies proving the safety and the benefits of the drugs. To me, the benefit of expanding public access to them was obvious. For example, many people who can't afford regular doctor visits still suffer from mild, common allergies. Of these allergy sufferers, many might need to drive a truck, study, or look after a child. The extant OTC antihistamines at the time, such as Benadryl, could cause severe drowsiness.

As a morning full of charts and graphs cycled by on the projection screen, my thoughts often drifted back to Andrew. Before long, a whole different debate was replaying inside my mind. I wholeheartedly opposed Andrew being medicated, but a concerted team of experts put Mary and me in a position with no viable alternative. There was no handbook to consult; we could only do our best to weigh the factors, and to put trust in the experts. Andrew was disrupting his class—not staying in his chair, failing to concentrate, and not finishing assignments. Though his teachers raved to us about his playfulness and sense of humor, apparently the higher priority was order in the classroom. What a highly subjective measure, I thought, for children of Andrew's age.

The wealth of data filling slide after slide at the conference only flamed my frustration. Why wasn't there a similarly robust cache of data available for the effects of Ritalin on young children?

After the insurers finished, presentations by the drug companies snapped me back to my surroundings. A parade of my former colleagues came across the podium to present disaster scenarios and a crush of, at best, tangentially related study data. The advisory panel, a group of FDA-selected doctors, sat impassively listening and occasionally being called upon to play referee.

The day progressed, and the angles of the presentations gradually became more obvious and more strident. Underneath the strenuous and willful obfuscation, it was all so simple—like the barnyard characters in Andrew's favorite book as a toddler. The drug reps were foxes, seeking only to maximize value for their shareholders. They would use any trick to keep their $3 billion prescription market intact. The insurance presenters were hens in the henhouse, their shareholders heavily insulated by legal regulations, but squawking and pecking through the fence at $800 million in new feed for their bottom lines. The doctors on the panel, paid to advise the FDA, were the wise owls, aloof but also territorial.

The final drug company presenter clicked shut his PowerPoint and faced the panel for questions, but none came. He quietly returned to his seat, and I felt my pulse quicken. Soon it would be my turn to speak. The complete absence of questions from the panel told me that no one was convinced by anything he had to say. From my seat, I actually overheard a doctor remark to a colleague, under his breath, "Unbelievably disingenuous."

The sound of my name being called choked me with a thick stew of thoughts and emotions. Andrew was at the front of my mind, and after a long morning listening to misdirection and muddying tactics, my patience was spent. I opened my notes, but was compelled instead to speak extemporaneously. I did my best to maintain my calm while I pointed out the holes in the presentations of the drug reps. I was brimming with contempt, but trying diplomatically and professionally to identify for the panel the obvious agendas at stake. I was sick of the attention everyone was forced to pay to massaged charts and data, so I skipped through my notes as quickly as possible.

"Here's the bottom line as far as I'm concerned," I said to conclude. "These non-sedating antihistamines have been available without prescription for many years in twenty-four other countries without a single mishap. Countries like Canada, Sweden, Denmark, the U.K., Australia, Germany, and Holland, all with highly respected government review boards on safety and efficacy, have approved these drugs' over-the-counter use."[1]

I looked to the panel and saw a row of smiles. After the deluge of unlikely scenarios and obscure, massaged numbers, I'd rebutted the long and winding arguments of the wealthy drug companies in two sentences.

"Thank you, Mr. Francesco," the committee head replied after looking around for questions.

I sat down under the heated stares of several former colleagues. I felt a high, momentarily empowered against the invisible and lurking forces I feared had breached my family's guard. The panel voted at the end of the day, based upon all it had seen and heard, that the non-sedating antihistamines were appropriate for non-prescription status.

As I rode the train home that night, I still felt the high. Our system is far from perfect, I thought to myself, but real life is lived in gray areas. The doctors had overwhelmingly voted in favor of OTC status. The hard, collected evidence proved these drugs' safe usage beyond a reasonable doubt. I felt my first real hope that equivalent data and diligence would eventually prove Dr. Pinketty right. Perhaps the medicine would nudge Andrew into better habits and help him progress toward a better-adjusted future. I wasn't naïve—professional experience and my responsibility to my family wouldn't allow it. But maybe, I thought for the first time, maybe I could let the medical professionals and experienced school administrators for once have the benefit of the doubt.

I watched lights pass outside the train window and felt calm.

It was a heated day, but the cool heads of the doctors were able to resist the overhyped interests, able to resist the unethical but easily overwhelming fear-baiting and distortions by the drug companies. When all was said and done, the public interest was well served.

My feelings lingered and helped buoy me straight through to November, when the FDA announced its final decision on the matter: to *reject* the petition to switch non-sedating antihistamines from Rx to OTC status. Incidental to the recommendation of the Rockville panel, the FDA's own lawyers had declared that it lacked the legal authority to force a switch in the first place.

CHAPTER FOUR

Flood Hill, Carving a New Path

South Orange, New Jersey
January 15, 2004

Six inches of snow blanketed everything in and around South Orange. Schools in the area were closed for two days, and Flood Hill, a town park, was swarmed with children. They were having a simply joyous time amid the double blessing of no school and gobs of fresh white stuff. I'd given myself an afternoon off work to take Andrew and his new plastic snowboard, a Christmas gift, out for a spin.

Pure enjoyment had become more and more elusive with Andrew. There were increasing conflicts over his behavior at school, and more battling over the shifting labels his doctors had begun to toss up around it. Disagreements with the "experts" and the results of their recommendations had caused us all a long streak of grief and confusion. The pills were not helping Andrew fit in, and he had drifted further from the standard population socially and academically, but the fresh snow was a sudden equalizer and a wonderful, rare touch of "normal" life. Here, he was in his element. Gliding over the frozen white canvas, Andrew was just one of the kids, bundled up and buzzing with excitement for winter fun. I was just another one of the dads at the bottom of the hill, jockeying for position with my video camera.

Andrew stood atop the hill, strapping back into his board. Shouting and laughter filled the cold air. The hill was a hive of activity as kids charged up and down with saucers, sleds, skis, and snowboards. Andrew was doing splendidly. He continually amazed me with his coordination. After just a few minutes of finding his balance, he completed his first run all the way from top to bottom without falling. I filmed Andrew as he hiked back to the top. With a hop he launched down the hill, managing the board, the snow, and the occasional human obstruction beautifully. He was almost fearless now. With each run he grew more confident. He stood up straighter and did more turning as he increased his feel for the board, the snow, and his remarkable God-given abilities. A former professional baseball player once visited our house and remarked, watching Andrew skateboard in our driveway, that his coordination was "one in ten thousand."

It was easy in such a moment to forget the string of incidents at school. Waiting just outside of this snowy oasis, there was a constant and lurking pressure on our family. Despite all our best efforts, Andrew's behavior at school had grown frighteningly out of control. Nothing we or his teachers and counselors tried seemed to improve it.

Here, though, he was free to express himself, to team up with gravity and overcome the challenges of the terrain, to feel the cold air blasting across his sweaty, smiling face. I felt such a thrill for him, and for myself, too. My son was a great athlete! And he made it look so effortless. At school, Andrew tried hard to be a "good kid," but he constantly got into trouble. There was something about the confinement of the school environment that could set him off.

In October, I'd been called to pick him up before noon when he refused to come inside from recess. He had started madly running around outside, and two young male teachers had to physically chase him down and force him back inside. Andrew was immediately put in detention, at a desk in the office next to the school principal, whom we had come to call Sergeant Smith. She had a famous catchphrase that she must have said thousands of times to errant children: "You have a choice. You don't need to behave this way."

Andrew was impulsive, and, when reprimanded, he would sit and sulk like it was an injustice. He was incapable of public contrition. In private, though, after reflection, it seemed like he knew that he'd made a mistake and regretted it. There were moments I remember clearly when, taking him away from school, I could actually see his self-esteem sinking in real time.

I'd been interacting with Sergeant Smith more and more over the school year, and I was running out of things to say to her. She would simply go to her refrain: "He has a choice." One time Andrew had refused to stop jumping on his chair. Another time, someone showed him how to shoot spitballs, and he immediately sent one at his teacher. My own frustration compounded the

problems; he would not respond to logic or to discipline. I tried
to consider that, in the moment, it was possible Andrew could
not see the imminent consequences of his actions. Either way, the
situation at school was clearly coming to a head. Andrew found
himself again and again in detention, next to Sergeant Smith, left
to ponder the words: "You have a choice."

Andrew's medication regimen had also ballooned well beyond the first Ritalin dose, which I had fought so hard against.
Gradually, over two years, Mary and I had caved in and yielded to
the pharmaceutical approach. Andrew's behavior had pushed us
further against a wall. The professional influence we felt from his
school, his counselors, and his doctors cohesively supported the
drug approach.

Andrew was not a bad kid. He behaved much better at home,
in fact. Mary and I did our best to advocate for him in various
meetings at school. The administration initiated an Individual
Education Plan (IEP) committee to monitor his behavior and
create reports and recommendations. I came to understand that
the committee meant well, but lacked the desire and proper resources to deal with Andrew's problems head-on and provide sug-
gestions. Their allegiance was ultimately to the order, harmony,
and discipline of the school at large. It forced Mary and me to play
diplomat, always open and prepared, but tenacious in protecting
our son. The most effective methods in these scenarios were to
establish early intervention on problems, to create a collaborative
tone, and to quickly identify and stay ahead of emerging threats to
Andrew's best interests. It became a very lonely job for us.

The IEP meeting after the spitball incident was attended by
educators and administrators, as well as mental health and social
workers. Sergeant Smith was at the helm, and, beyond the basic
drive for overall order at the school, there were additional unspo-

ken stakes. Andrew had been placed in a special education classroom. It was the first year that the school had established a special education class, and a lot was riding on its success. Apparently the district was attempting to save a large sum of money by running this class "in-house" instead of paying a much higher per-student rate to ship their special needs kids out of district. I knew that Sergeant Smith had a special needs child of her own, and I added appeals to her empathy into my game plan for the meeting. The large attendance roster was supposed to be proof of the district-wide interest in the future of this new classroom and its students. It was obvious that Sergeant Smith viewed Andrew's case as its biggest obstacle to success.

The meeting commenced, very polite at the surface level. Andrew's daily teacher in the special education classroom was a recent graduate and new hire. She gave her report on Andrew's behavior and repeated the list of disruptive and rule-breaking incidents. We heard from the other professionals present about their concerns for Andrew and his progress through the curriculum. Andrew was behind and falling further. It was apparent to me that, given Andrew's own mounting distaste and disgruntlement, there was no light at the end of the tunnel.

The professionals at the meeting represented very different areas of expertise. I noticed how the administrators' broad goals were often a source of friction against the more individual goals reported by the social workers. Medication, however, seemed to be the great uniting force. Sometimes in IEP meetings a counselor or teacher would push for a change to Andrew's medication. Sometimes an administrator would pointedly suggest that I schedule a new consultation with Andrew's psychiatrist. And both blocs seemed entirely pleased whenever they heard that Andrew had had a change to his medication cocktail. Tinkering with his medication was always received as a satisfyingly definitive and immediate action. Everybody bought into the medication plan.

But the reality to me seemed very different. Instead of purposeful action with an expectation of progress, the course of treatment from Andrew's psychiatrist—a good man—seemed more or less arbitrary. It was clear that Andrew was emotionally troubled and suffering, but there was never a lasting or convincing evidence-based diagnosis. Each diagnosis and corresponding change to his medication came across as a speculative attempt: "Let's see if this works." Complicating matters further, the school's behavior reports factored heavily into the diagnoses. Andrew's teachers, counselors, and administrators actually played a significant part in the medication program—all beating the pharmaceutical drum.

Home from Flood Hill, Andrew went to his room to change into dry clothes and rest. I was still riding high on the mini-vacation from work and from the stress of battling both for and with Andrew. It had been a great day, and I had gotten great footage of Andrew on the hill. I was excited to show Mary and brought it up on the camera's display screen while she cooked dinner.

Mary had spoken with the school's psychologist, Dr. Zurick, while we were out. He was very generous to call us from home on a snow day. I liked Dr. Zurick. He was diligent and helpful—and very overworked, I suspected.

"He told me there are other schools in the area with special-ed setups that may work better for Andrew," she said. "But we'd need approval from the superintendent of schools for Andrew to go outside the South Orange system."

"Great!" I said. "Let's do it. I feel like we're running into a wall with the public schools."

"He also said that the superintendent is unlikely to grant the request now that they've invested in doing special ed themselves."

"We'll do what it takes," I said, visions of Andrew weaving art-fully down the slope still playing in my mind. "Do any of the other schools look interesting?"

"Who knows?" she sighed. "All the schools have websites, but how can you really tell if they're any good? How do you even know if you've searched all the schools and not just a few? There's no master list."

"What about reviews or reports for the schools?"

"Just anecdotal from the school psychologist or the social worker. And they all say the only way to really tell is to take An-drew to meet the staff. They'd have to interview Andrew as well, to see if they want him." Mary's face was tense. I wished there was something I could do to relieve her.

It was time for Andrew's evening medication, and I took his weekly pill dispenser off the counter. Throughout the saga of changing medications, I'd created a chart that listed the condi-tions and intended purpose for each drug. It gave me a tiny feeling of control in an otherwise overwhelming situation.

MEDICATION	PURPOSE	NOTES
2/11/03 Strattera 25 mg, 1x in the AM. Add in PM in 2 weeks: Catapres 0.1 mg, 1/2 tab 3x/day.	Diagnosis from Pinketty: ADHD, combined type; ODD, OCD, Maybe Tourette's syndrome. 2nd psych. Dr. Keenen diagnosis, all the above and need to rule out mood disorder.	Transition to 2nd child psychiatrist, Dr. Keenen. No more prescriptions from pediatrician or Dr. Pinketty. Andrew angry a lot, low self-esteem, daydream-ing, talking back, poor concentration.
8/2/03 Added Zoloft 12.5 mg once per day.	Pills not doing anything.	Swearing is growing, every day now.

MEDICATION	PURPOSE	NOTES
9/26/03 Upped Zoloft to 50 mg, added clonidine 0.1 mg 3x/day. No more Strattera, Catapres.	Andrew said to Mary, "Touch my penis," "Smack my butt." Mimicking Austin Powers in Goldmember?	Dr. Keenen notes, "No psycho/social support" for patient in public school classroom.
10/28/03 Lowered Zoloft to 25 mg.	Jumping off chairs.	Suspended 3 times now, Again no psycho/social support from school system.
12/3/03 Added Trileptal 300 mg.	New IEP. Another new Dr. Keenen diagnosis: bipolar, ADHD, OCD.	Spitballs may have hit teacher. Extra Trileptal drug may stabilize mood.

Zoloft and clonidine were not approved by the FDA for treatment of children; they were off-label prescriptions.[1] Yet there they were under the blue flaps, waiting to be fed to Andrew. The medication management approach had taken the form of target shooting, spraying bullets at various and sundry symptoms. He had a new macro-diagnosis: bipolar disorder. But the medication management approach for ten year-old Andrew seemed unfortunately similar to the neurologist's proposal when Andrew might have had epilepsy at three: "Try this medication and see if it changes anything." We had rejected this approach before. And it didn't help to build our faith that Andrew's diagnoses seemed to change drastically every few months.

The stress and frustration for his two very diligent parents was significant. There were no definitively positive results from any of Andrew's medications—hence the constant changes. We also had no idea what lasting side effects these drugs could be causing.

None among the collection of experts could truly verify any benefit from the battery of medications. The only changes in Andrew that we could register for sure were tics, twitching, fatigue, and new manic behavior.

Could the medication management concept protect against a gradual buildup of drugs in the system that could ultimately hurt Andrew? There was no blood testing, for example, to track his physiological responses to new medications. The doctors relied on clinical feel for the subject only. And throughout, there was almost no mention of alternative treatments, even classics such as talk therapy.[2] When did this approach change? I'd always thought that psychiatry was a blend of art and science, utilizing a variety of approaches like analysis and cognitive therapy. The focus in 2003, however, seemed locked onto the tweaking of prescriptions.

Had the profession changed at large? Andrew's doctors prescribed each drug with full confidence, despite their readily admitted "trial and error" philosophy. Every failed attempt seemed to leave them unfazed. The children's mental health field has maintained the guise of treating disease based upon hard science,[3] with proven and repeatable inputs and outputs, but Andrew's four years of medication had no such results. Studies have actually shown that we used to expect better results in psychiatry when combining drug therapy with talk or other alternative methods. The "alternative" approach, it seemed, had become merely to try an alternative drug.

The predominant players in the children's mental health industry have morphed it into a dedicated drug market. This outcome is not surprising in our for-profit health care system. Rather than a patient, my son was viewed as a consumer statistic, spinning through drugs as if he were trying different soda flavors. Incentives for insurers, drug makers, and school institutions all point in an unfortunately similar direction. I wanted to have faith that the medicines were helping Andrew. As someone who built a career around the marketing of pharmaceuticals, I believed strongly in the industry's overall mission. Still, I had never worked in children's mental health. Andrew's treatment struck me as simplistic, narrow-minded, and filled with magical thinking. Unfortunately, despite huge industry advances in oncology, cardiovascular, allergy, etc., the Francesco family was stuck treading water in the most important category for us: mental health.

And, meanwhile, Andrew was slipping further away from the possibility of a normal experience at school. Without definitive test results or diagnoses, and without clear benefits to point to from Andrew's increasing list of medications, Mary and I had begun to feel like desperate gamblers stuck at a cold table, re-upping and waiting for our luck to change.

CHAPTER FIVE

On the Beach at Rockport

Rockport, Massachusetts
August 25, 2004

*M*y son is handicapped.

That phrase ricocheted inside my head as I sat on the beach with my family on a much-needed vacation from work and the simmering pressure that Andrew had brought to our lives. I watched Andrew turn perfect cartwheels along the shoreline. He went back and forth in the wet sand, pulling ten or more in a row before coming to a flawless stop, feet together and hands at his sides like a competing gymnast. Strangers walking the beach actually stopped to watch his performance. The joy he derived from exercising his physical command, along with the smell of fresh air and feel of the sand, was palpable. I hadn't seen him that free and uninhibited since our great day together at Flood Hill.

In February, I'd begun to visit a psychologist to help myself better manage the pressures of our situation. "Steve, you realize that your son is handicapped, don't you?" she said during our second session together.

I was struck speechless.

"What? I'm not sure you're right about that," I stammered.

"It's clear that he is considered handicapped by the state. Otherwise he wouldn't have been approved for the out-of-district transfer."

Andrew was due to begin at The Smithwick School, outside the official South Orange public school district, in two weeks. The initiative to transfer him had been supported by Sergeant Smith and the rest of the administration.

"Yes, but . . . I mean, he has social issues . . ."

"Andrew is considered to be handicapped. I'm surprised that no one has expressed that to you before."

During his last half-year in the South Orange school, he'd developed even more problems with uncontrolled outbursts. At home, I'd also witnessed ten-year-old Andrew's behavior take a turn for the worse. I could actually see two sides playing out a battle sometimes inside his mind. He would say in an otherwise calm moment, "Mom, can we go to the poopy—I mean park! Park!" I heard him yell at himself while he played video games. Sometimes he would call himself stupid and punch himself in the chin—the same boy who could be so charming and physically talented.

The counselors at South Orange had taught him a series of tactics to help control his behavior. It seemed like he did his best to arm himself with these tactics when he felt the urges taking over.

I'd heard Andrew in the kitchen with Mary the previous week having a casual talk when he suddenly veered off, mid-sentence: "Mom, what the fuck . . . I mean fucking . . . I mean, not fucking, freaking. No, not freaking either! I mean what the freak! No! Not that either! OK. OK. I'm done."

Mary was taken aback. Before she could respond, Andrew went into repentant mode. "Mom, just before, when I said the F-word, I really didn't mean to. OK? OK? I'm done. Five, four, three, two, one, negative one." One of the tactics was to count backwards silently whenever he felt himself losing control. "Oh, I did the counting thing out loud! I didn't mean to! OK, OK. I'm done!"

Back on the beach, Andrew dove in between Mary and me. She was reading a book in a beach chair next to mine. He rolled around, feeling the warm sand on his ocean-cooled skin, and looked up at us with a puppy-dog face. Mary stared harder into the pages of her book. She was on near constant edge around Andrew. The work she did defending Andrew was compounded by the work she did to defend herself from Andrew. Back at home after a grueling IEP meeting, for example, she would often be subjected to further outbursts and sexual references from Andrew. She had to cope with comments about her body parts and criticisms over mysterious offenses like going barefoot in the house.

Mary had created a complicated array of reward and punishment systems for Andrew to help stem his behavior and better organize his thinking. I could see that her engagement with him had become dangerously costly to her. Over Christmas vacation, she had actually been so depressed that she confined herself to bed for four days. She would ask me over and over, despairingly, "Is this what our life is going to be like?" before catching herself and switching to a declarative tone of voice to say, "This is what our life is like." It broke my heart. Her love for Andrew was unlimited, but had a cost. She would end each dip into despair with a genuine, optimistic question: "What else can we do? There must be other options."

Meanwhile, between us, Andrew pawed at the sand, carrying through his puppy dog routine. In his deep brown eyes I could see pure joy and peace. It was a rare and fleeting moment of harmony between us. I was thrilled to see him so happy. Over this week at the beach, Andrew had spent hours just lying in the wet sand and saltwater tide pools, peacefully soaking up the surroundings, thinking his thoughts, and feeling his feelings.

The vacation had done a lot to restore the whole family. Margaux had also suffered a lot from Andrew's behavior. Just spending time around the house was often difficult for her. When Andrew was in the room, he could quickly suck all the air out. So much centered around him and his needs, and Margaux could easily be pushed offstage. Since Mary spent so much of her energy dealing with Andrew, I tried to relieve her whenever I could find time away from work.

This routine robbed my daughter of a huge amount of time and attention from me as her father. I felt so many sad moments pass when I knew that I should have been with her, talking and listening to her challenges and worries instead. She showed tremendous individual strength and high standards, and I too often took these for granted. I prioritized Andrew, Mary, and my business—and to this day I feel guilty.

It came to be that Andrew ran the show. He was an incredible mass of contradictions. He was so talented physically, yet so troubled socially. Between his obsessive behaviors and violent, disruptive outbursts, he could be incredibly sweet and funny. We all loved him with heart and soul, and it was sometimes easy to forget that he too was trying very hard just to get along. Throughout his young life he had endured criticisms and deep inner challenges. Every morning he would rise and greet a world that was a great source of friction for him, ready to do his best to make progress—to absorb the guidance from his teachers, counselors, administrators, doctors, counselors, social workers, family, and, strangely, even the calmer sides of himself.

He'd been through a lot over the previous two years. The whole family had. I was still processing all these worries at the beach, but I knew I was deeply troubled by Andrew's upcoming school change. Could I accept that Andrew wouldn't ever be like the normal kids? Was there still a glimmer of hope that the ever-growing collection of experts and professionals were somehow wrong about him? Inside I still carried the hope that we'd eventually uncover some elusive answer—the right placement, or the right guidance, or, yes, the right medicine that could set him back on track. Seeing Andrew free to play on the beach buoyed my hope that there was something undiscovered out there that could deliver him.

There'd been a pretty drastic change of course with Andrew's medications almost a year before: the addition of antipsychotics. Before introducing the mood stabilizers and antidepressants, Andrew's child psychiatrist had kept him on a shifting combination of stimulants (Ritalin, Concerta, Adderall) and a sleep aid (Catapres) to counteract them at night. The new drug class, however, had thrown an additional degree of uncertainty and a higher chemical potency into the mix, as well as an expanding list of potentially dangerous side effects. Drugs can react differently according to the individual body and brain chemistries of patients. The medication management program was there to keep an eye out for potentially damaging contingencies, thankfully.

But after almost a year, we'd again detected little if any positive change in Andrew's behavior. I trusted the prescribers to be well-intentioned, and I desired deeply to believe in the medication's eventual efficacy. I felt pressed thin from work, from playing steady advocate, and from being a husband and father. I had precious little energy left in reserve and wished for more comfort from the experts, but the lack of scientific rigor I perceived around the application of these atypical antipsychotic drugs gave me steady pause. Working with antihistamine drugs was drastically different: a hay fever allergy diagnosis is simple, the results or lack of results from drugs were obvious, and the chemical mechanism of the drug was well understood.

Andrew's new brain meds were far more potent and much less well understood from a clinical standpoint. From my research on the Internet, it became clear that even psychiatric experts held different theories about why they allegedly worked or did not work. There were some doctors who broke ranks and wrote articles protesting the current practice of medicating so many children with these new and expensive drugs.[1]

An extreme multi-dose of the allergy drug Claritin, by comparison, was far less potentially damaging than tiny doses of various medications in Andrew's regimen. Each change or addition to his regimen was a new roll of the dice. Andrew's young body coursed with chemicals that advertised potential side effects like difficulty walking, tremors, facial tics, stuttering, obesity, and more. And, so far, none of the drugs had come close to bringing Andrew peace of mind or calm—not even a hint at how he seemed to feel while free to roam and play on the beach.

Anticipating his major school change, Andrew was on the following medication schedule:

DRUG	DOSAGE AND ADMINISTRATION	DESCRIPTION FOR ANDREW'S NEEDS
Risperdal	1.25 mg @ 7:15 AM, 0.5 mg @ 3:15 PM & 7:30 PM	Atypical antipsychotic to straighten out thinking, slow down behavior
Concerta	36 mg once per day	Stimulant to help focus; can make you jittery
Trileptal	450 mg twice per day	Mood stabilizer to keep emotions under control better
Catapres	0.1 mg at bedtime	Sleep inducer just before bed
Luvox	25 mg twice per day	Antidepressant to try to avoid down moments

In my own mind, I couldn't negotiate how there were really no discernible effects in Andrew's behavior, given all this medication at work in his system. Watching him on the beach, I wondered what his behavior might be if we pulled him off all the drugs completely. In the context of school or regular family life, how much worse could it even get?

Mary made us dinner that night in the happy bubble of our rental house. Even with the tension from Andrew's unpredictable mood swings and outbursts, we enjoyed the solace. Away from work, away from responsibility, away from the never-ceasing phone calls and discipline for Andrew, we were able to just be a family together. Andrew stayed in a good mood all through the meal. Mary and I even had a chance to reprise some long-lost, private looks across the table. For a time we all felt settled, just tasting food and being together.

Driving home the next day, our car was filled with beach air, toys, and luggage. On the surface, things appeared the same as they had returning from any of our previous vacations. We even tried singing together on the car ride, but there was something different—less heart and less abandon to it. We were more conscious of our roles in a family united around an increasingly challenged child. We struggled to find the lighthearted harmony on the way home from vacation that was still alive in our memories.

I had also begun to worry for myself around this time. I worried about my own ability to stay on top of things. I had begun to feel what is called decision fatigue.[2] Psychologists recognize this as a common condition in people who have endured a long series of complicated and unclear choices. A common end result of decision fatigue is to gradually yield control and give in to events. After too many challenging choices, the decision maker can become less effective in analysis and more prone to error. I had been barraged with decisions about Andrew's well-being nonstop for years, and wondered how much I was slipping. How much of my relatively clear thought and analysis—something I felt I was good at—had I surrendered to events and influences with regard to Andrew's medication? Could simple exhaustion have affected our choice to accept his transfer?

Looking back now, I see hidden levers that altered the foundation on which we had to make our decisions. Andrew was diagnosed with emerging bipolar disorder as part of his medication change, but I was not sure if Andrew's symptoms really aligned with what I read about it online. I went back and forth in my mind. True, Andrew could become easily agitated, angry, or demanding one minute, and then relatively happy the next. However, the swings seemed to occur faster than the swings described in the articles on the Internet. When he was angry, there was always a reason. Andrew showed other high-intensity symptoms as well. He could become physically threatening without warning. We had actually hidden the house knives a few months before when Andrew got uncomfortably deep into a horror movie he saw. Mary was afraid that he might lose track of fantasy versus reality and actually hurt someone.[3]

The symptoms of bipolar disorder were related to a diagnosis known by the previous generation as manic depression. Having a name for something gives the feeling of control, but how did our psychiatrist get to this diagnosis?

At the time, I didn't fully account for the fact that the doctor needed a diagnostic classification in order to issue certain prescriptions and continue billing our insurance company for Andrew's visits. The insurance companies prefer easily schedulable expenses that correspond with a certain diagnosis: x number of psychiatrist visits per year, and x dollars for medication reimbursements. The classifications help them to organize these schedules. If the doctor believes that a certain treatment or medication course might benefit a patient, it is in his interest to attach a corresponding diagnosis. The classifications can seem vague, but they enable doctors to use their full tool kit—especially for psychiatric disorders that carry broad or relatively subjective symptoms. But whom did the classification of bipolar disorder actually benefit the most: our insurance company, Dr. Keenen, or Andrew? And in what direction did it pull us with regard to Andrew's treatment?

CHAPTER SIX

Turning Outside the District for Relief

September 4, 2004

Dropping Andrew off for the first time at Smithwick hit me harder than expected. It felt as if we were surrendering the fight for him to ever lead a normal life. The realization hadn't fully landed for me before, and it was enormously difficult to accept that my eleven-year-old son needed a special school.

Andrew was buzzing in the front passenger seat when we arrived. I could read his deep and tragic desire to fit in somewhere—to feel like a basically functional and responsible person, just like he saw his sister doing up close every day. We all hoped for relief from the constant pummeling stress that Andrew both caused and received while in the South Orange school system. Along with the new medication regimen, he was also armed with a terrific new private psychologist, Dr. Ferry, to help guide him.

As Andrew grew bigger and progressed through the South Orange school system, the burden of supervising him had grown close to unbearable. He was sent home from school more and more frequently. The new and complex mix of medications Andrew was taking continued to eat at me, but the first day at Smithwick was a chance for a clean slate—the complicated and well orchestrated result of guidance from experts in education, counseling, and medicine. Mary and I took some comfort in the knowledge that we had done all we could in the search for answers, even though real progress for Andrew had continued to elude us. He was so naturally talented in so many ways, yet so challenged in basic daily operations that most of us take for granted.

I had a heavy heart watching Andrew disappear into the school. Smithwick was considered an alternative special education school, one with lower academic expectations and a far more flexible and supportive attitude than the South Orange public school system and Sergeant Smith. The attending children suffered from a range of mild intellectual and emotional challenges.

The placement, however, was not a success for Andrew. There was an awkward adjustment period for both sides, and his acting out continued. With the best help from our private psychologist, Dr. Ferry, and our private psychiatrist, Dr. Keenen, as well as the school staff, Andrew was still unable to make any basic social connections. We all stumbled forward during his first year there. It wasn't easy, but it got done. Sometimes you can become resigned to just getting by.

Andrew struggled into a second year there. Entering the sixth grade in September of 2005, he fell even further behind academically, and his frustrations seemed to grow in concert. Instead of any relief from the out-of-district school switch, everything that we did as a family had come to be colored or outright limited by Andrew's behavior. The Francesco family was in a box.

I walked into the kitchen one early fall evening while Mary helped Andrew with his homework and saw Andrew hit and curse himself. "Stupid! Stupid!" he yelled. It seemed to take every fiber of his being to hold back his erupting energy and try to channel it into his work. Mary stood saintly by and did her best to absorb and redirect.

His misbehavior at school began to escalate further in December. He believed very strongly that his teacher disliked him. I hoped that the Christmas break would be a useful respite and he could return in January a calmer Andrew. No such luck. Andrew's stress had triggered a major bout of obsessive-compulsive disorder (OCD).

Around the house, he became locked into behaviors like straightening out the fringe around the edge of an Oriental carpet or touching the same light switch panel over and over. He even personified his OCD attacks and would shout out sometimes, "OCD, I hate you! I hate you! Stop!" He was captured by his inner demon and found it difficult to escape from its clutches.

Desperate to help him and out of options, we asked Dr. Keenen for a medication switch two weeks before twelve-year-old Andrew was due back at Smithwick for the new term. Was our request even reasonable? Looking back, I see that I had stopped second-guessing the medication approach. Over time, our exhaustion and the layers of habit building around Andrew's expanding list of medications had led us to turn over responsibility to the drug god in the sky and the psychiatrist on the ground. We were grasping at anything that could deliver any bit of progress or control over the situation. I realize now that Dr. Keenen was also working to manage us, as Andrew's suffering and striving parents.

We became willing to make riskier choices, with even more off-label attempts. The majority of psychiatric drugs prescribed to children in 2007, in fact, were off-label.[1] Winning FDA approval is especially difficult for pediatric populations—and very expensive. Off-label prescribing is a relatively unregulated source of psychiatric drugs for kids in the U.S. If a drug supposedly works for adults, then why not try a smaller dosage for children? The approach tragically fails to consider that the fragile and developing brain chemistry of a child might be materially different from the brain chemistry of a fully-grown adult.

A few of Andrew's drugs subsequently won FDA approval for children, but only for more severe mental illnesses like schizophrenia. Even with approval, however, there is a good chance that these potent psycho-pharmaceuticals were not tested for lasting developmental side effects.

Drug makers are strictly forbidden to promote off-label uses of their products in this country, yet they continue to do so despite billions of dollars in fines. Where is the logic here? The U.S. prescribes psychiatric medications to children at a rate three to four times higher than other scientifically sophisticated countries.[2]

Medicine is a constantly evolving field, but the U.S. health care system is largely constructed around potential conflicts of interest. Drug companies are very skilled at both spreading and obscuring data in accordance with their agendas. Our for-profit system highly incentivizes drug reps and marketers to open new markets for their existing products. Sales reps will covertly mention off-label uses to doctors, for example. The tactics can grow much more savvy, elaborate, and subtle from there.

Per our request to help with his OCD and anxiety, Dr. Keenen prescribed Andrew Klonopin and an increased dosage of Zoloft, both off-label, before he returned to school in January. I trusted Dr. Keenen's intentions implicitly. We saw him at least once every four weeks, and he kept an exceptionally close and caring eye on Andrew. But how can I be sure that biased reports or even outright illegal promotion did not subtly influence his decisions to prescribe? Since many of the drugs were still relatively new, how much data was even available?

When Andrew boarded his bus for the first day back at Smithwick after winter vacation, I breathed a sigh of relief and headed over to my home office. A little quiet time to focus solely on my work was much needed. Around noon, however, Smithwick called to say that I needed to come and retrieve Andrew immediately.

I drove on Route 10, parallel to South Orange Avenue, past low-slung offices and strip malls, on my way to get him. Dingy signs for doctors' offices and medical facilities leapt out at me along the way, competing for my concentration. Smithwick had been very tolerant and understanding with Andrew, but I was beginning to worry that he could be kicked out.

Walking through the school's main entrance, I was struck additionally with sympathy for Andrew's teachers and the other staff who had to deal with his increasingly defiant and aggressive behavior. Mrs. Chandler, one of the social workers, was the first to greet me inside the administrative office. She looked upset and began speaking quickly.

"Mr. Francesco, we had a great deal of trouble with Andrew today. He was unmanageable. Andrew's behavior on the bus this morning was difficult for the driver. The driver had to call Mrs. Jamison over to the bus to discuss what he was doing—banging on the ceiling of the bus, yelling at the kids when he got off, and saying, 'Goodbye, losers!'

"Andrew entered the building with a negative attitude and

displayed his anger by yelling at Mrs. Jamison. He was unwilling to follow our direction. It took a lot of coaxing and discussion to finally have Andrew follow through with going to his class to check in.

"At 10:15, Andrew left the classroom, came back to Mrs. Jamison's time-out room, had a snack, and tried to remain focused on his work. He became agitated easily and tried asking for help from Mrs. Jamison. However, the math seemed to be too demanding for him. He made a comment about being tired, and Mrs. Jamison suggested that he put his head down. Although that option was given to him, he continued to become verbally aggressive. From that time, about 11:00, he was unmanageable."

I'd heard variations of this report before. Mrs. Chandler told me that they wanted Andrew out of the building—she couldn't say for how long. I started to feel sick, a familiar ache spreading through my gut, and I knew a headache was close behind it. But Mrs. Chandler wasn't finished.

"Andrew made comments about wanting to hurt himself, kill himself. He ripped his book, threw a pencil across the room. He threw a book, charged across the room screaming when Mrs. Jamison and I were trying to close the door, and he shoved over the video camera and broke it."

I interjected that I would pay for the camera, but she continued without pausing or acknowledging.

"I needed to call Dr. Bennett to come to Mrs. Jamison's room. Andrew continued to take the ripped pieces of paper off the floor and throw them at Dr. Bennett. He was rolling around on his back, jumping up and throwing himself into the wall. He ripped down a poster from the wall and began licking his hands. He said insulting things to Dr. Bennett, Mrs. Jamison, and myself. He was passing gas purposely and expressing that as he did so.

"Mr. Francesco, the level of intervention that Andrew needed today was beyond our capability. We needed to place all of the other students outside of Mrs. Jamison's room. In addition, we do not have a quiet room for Andrew to go to when these behaviors flare up as they did today. Frankly, we are unable to maintain him in his current state. You need to keep Andrew home until we have time to hear back from Andrew's psychiatrist on what kind of interventions can be applied to help Andrew. We need to see what other options may work for Andrew for him to be successful. He's sitting in the nurse's office now waiting for you."

When she finished, I looked up from the floor. "I'm so sorry everyone had so much trouble with Andrew today," I said. "He's been having a rough time at school since before Christmas. I don't really know why."

"Well," she said, straightening her back, "he is suspended until we are more clear on how or whether we can manage him and help him be a success."

"I understand," I said, and turned to leave the office.

As I walked down the hallway, another of the senior staff, Mr. Archibald, approached me. "Mr. Francesco, may I have a moment?"

I stopped to face him, my mind solely on Andrew waiting alone in the nurse's office.

"Mr. Francesco," he began, "I do consulting work outside of school with people who have gone through serious traumas. I feel compelled to tell you that I've seen Andrew exhibit similar symptoms to some of my trauma patients. I believe his anxiety level at school is way too high for him to be able to function. He has an inability to cope with simple everyday school events. His confidence and self-esteem are extremely low, and he is very depressed. He really cannot afford more traumatic days here at school."

I simply didn't know what to say at this point.

"He needs immediate changes, pharmacologic as well as coping mechanisms, in a supportive environment, in order to get him back on track. As you know, we cannot do that here."

It was increasingly clear that Smithwick lacked the appropriate programs, facilities, or specialized training to help Andrew. In some ways, it was a glorified baby-sitting service with some education thrown in. Andrew had been on medication consistently ever since he started on Ritalin at eight. He took the ever-shifting daily regimen of pills dutifully, because he trusted us. These trips to pull him out of school only seemed to prove the approach was not successful—and may actually have been hurting him.

"Maybe you're right," I said abruptly to Mr. Archibald. "We'll need to talk to his psychiatrist and see what we can do. Thanks for your advice."

"Of course," he said.

I wheeled quickly around to where Andrew was waiting. I was overwhelmed by everything that was happening. He never grew so out of control at home.

Andrew was sitting in a chair flipping a magazine when I opened the door to the nurse's office. He kept his head down at the sound of the door.

"Hey, Andrew," I said, trying to sound as casual as possible.

When Andrew looked up at me, his eyes were bloodshot red. His face was pained, and I thought I could see tears begin to well up. Before any could fall, though, he threw the magazine down at his feet. "I hate this fucking place!" he screamed. "Get me out of here!"

"OK," I said. "Control your voice."

"I hate this fucking-fucking place!"

"You need to control your voice and language," I said. "We're going home now."

"Good!" he said, standing up.

I helped him slide on his backpack. I looked at him for a clue as to how difficult our ride home was going to be, but his expression was inscrutable. He sunk his head as we walked down the hallway and out to the parking lot, thankfully without passing any other kids or teachers.

Dr. Keenen emailed us this report a few days later, regarding the incident:

> Increasing Andrew's dose of the antidepressant Zoloft for mood stabilization from 25 mg to 50 mg might have activated and agitated him, while his new Klonopin prescription, which is intended for controlling seizures, might have sedated and irritated him. The combination of these two effects could have caused him to lose control.

I pictured Andrew on Mrs. Jamison's floor, desperately flailing and rolling on his back like a dog with an itch. It was another heartbreaking memory for his fragile psyche. I decided not to tell Mary about everything from that day. I felt an increasing need to protect her from some of the details—a major change from the past. We were both getting worn down, but she even more than me.

Mary and I tried to explain to Andrew later that though he ultimately had to be responsible for his behavior, there were chemicals affecting his body and brain that were beyond his control. I still wonder what Andrew was feeling inside his twelve-year-old body that day, with brand new hormones coursing alongside the medications in his blood. He was a chemical cauldron. Though Mary and I did our best to acquire every bit of technique and expert advice that was available to us as parents, somewhere along the way, Dr. Keenen the prescriber had become our main ally against Andrew's struggles and outbursts. Had we yielded too much territory?

For twenty years in the U.S., antidepressants have been pitched almost as casually as vitamin supplements—even as the actual wide-ranging and stand-alone efficacy of SSRIs (selective sero-tonin reuptake inhibitors) such as Prozac and Zoloft are highly debated. The serotonin addition was thought to raise the spirits. Unfortunately, most psychiatrists now feel that antidepressants do very little, except for the most seriously disturbed patients. They are still widely prescribed, however, largely because patients believe they can help and there are few major side effects. Antide-pressant use has become a deeply embedded narrative in our cul-ture, but do doctors have the responsibility to update the public?

The steep rise in chemical intervention in this country has co-incided with an overall decline in talk and other types of therapy, driven by incentives from the medical insurance industry. Po-tential effects of medication can be seen more quickly than the slower-building effects of therapy, and the lower predictable cost of monthly medications compared to talk or cognitive behavior therapy (CBT) is better business for insurers. But is it better for our children?

In the stress and confusion of caring for Andrew, the financial conflicts of interest within the children's mental health indus-try failed to fully materialize in my thinking. Mary and I had no trusted model to work with, only the limited real-time advice of the doctors. The Internet was becoming more useful, but who had time to dig through all the information? My visceral doubts over the medication path—beginning with Ritalin—were trampled down in the shuffle of day-to-day struggles with Andrew.

On a Sunday a little later in January, the Francesco family gath-ered in the living room to take down our Christmas tree. Andrew was still serving out his suspension from Smithwick, but was due back the next day, for what I assumed to be a final chance. We were all doing our best to create a normal holiday scene, with Mary and Margaux putting away the ornaments, per tradition.

Andrew was carefully lining up the red bulbs in a box. It was a rare moment of calm for him. His lingering embarrassment, pain, and self-loathing occupied my mind as we went through the motions of my favorite end-of-holiday ritual. I could see how upset he was, feeling that he was responsible for his bizarre behavior and scared by what awaited him back at school.

I felt helpless to protect my son. All I could do was pray.

With everyone peacefully on task, I stared at the bare tree. The Douglas fir had wonderful broad branches that lifted high up and out. Laden with ornaments and lights, it had become a unique and beautiful object. The decorations required the support of the tree to make their grace and harmony possible.

Andrew clearly required different or additional support, and I felt that, as his parents and advocates, we were failing him.

CHAPTER SEVEN

Lightning Strikes

January 2007

It was a clear and cold winter afternoon. Leaving the parking lot of Aventis, a major pharmaceutical client, I felt downcast, struck by an unfortunate development for my business. Aventis was the new name for two recently merged European drug companies, Rhône-Poulenc Rorer and Hoechst Marion Roussel. For the past five years, I'd been working with Hoechst to prepare an Rx-to-OTC switch for Allegra, their non-sedating antihistamine. However, the new Aventis personnel considered this a waste of time. Even with the competitive product, Claritin, due to make the switch to OTC, they just didn't care. They had little regard for the years of work done before their arrival or the potential financial consequences to the company.

My sense was that the unseen force of company culture had slapped down our long-brewing initiative without much consideration. To me, it didn't make sense. Insurance companies usually drop reimbursement for prescription drugs when an OTC alternative becomes available. Claritin switching to OTC was guaranteed to send prescription Allegra sales plummeting, and the OTC market could bring $300 million in annual sales with a 20% profit margin. Still, they didn't seem to care.

This new stance, though financially questionable, was politically correct within the new Aventis culture. They preferred to steer their time and resources toward launching new prescription drugs, which bring higher prices and profits, and can motivate armies of doctor-detailing salespeople. Diverting these resources was a higher-aiming career gamble for the ambitious executives, if one that came as a shock to me.

My team desperately wanted to stick with Aventis. We had invested a lot of work, and the money was good. Sitting in my car, I knew I was going to lose this business. Yet somehow I was more anxious about my next meeting, thirty minutes away.

For a year Andrew had attended a new drug- and therapy-oriented day school called The Wainwright Academy, and I was due for a required weekly meeting with their staff psychologist— something I'd begun to call "The Parental Punishment Hour." The Wainwright Academy was very different from Smithwick. It put a significant amount of focus on therapy: daily group sessions for the students and frequent individual counseling, as well as the required weekly parent discussions, sometimes with Andrew present. Wainwright was also affiliated with a well-known medical school. Going in, I felt that the place had a lot of promise.

Mary and I were very thorough in our research and, for better or worse, had become skilled at the process of finding new schools. We even employed the help of a finder: a wonderful older woman named Mrs. Lynch. Mrs. Lynch had gotten a law degree later in life and dedicated herself to helping children with school difficulties. She had extremely valuable experience and lots of sincere, objective advice.

On the way to Wainwright that day, though, with the sun shining off the salt-crusted pavement and gray snowbanks, my mind was swimming with dread.

I walked into the school, signed myself in, made a few turns, and sat down alone with Dr. Petrov in his cold and barren office. Mary and I had been fighting, and she refused to join me.

"Your son feels ashamed of himself," Dr. Petrov said, his voice flat and droning. He loved to drop bombs as a way to get your attention.

A downside of Wainwright was its strict policy banning contact with outside doctors and therapists, which meant we lost Andrew's great team of Dr. Keenen and Dr. Ferry. Though he was perhaps too casual about changing Andrew's diagnoses and medications, we liked Dr. Keenen. He really seemed to care and was deeply invested in Andrew's case. And Dr. Ferry was a truly rare find. He was an exceptionally talented therapist—a psychologist who was exceedingly knowledgeable about medications, schools, and the interdependent needs of kids and families. He got Andrew to talk like no one else ever did. He cut to the chase quickly on the right subjects and consistently found ways to reduce our family tensions. He was a sane island of safety and support in the turbulent and cold health care ocean, albeit one I had to pay for out-of-pocket. Dr. Ferry's care was not covered under my $1,600/month insurance policy.

Still, Wainwright appeared to be an ideal choice for Andrew. Their institutional approach was built around teaching each student an individualized set of coping skills. They performed a battery of tests on Andrew to identify specific deficiencies. We learned, for example, that Andrew was quicker to learn things that were spoken to him instead of read in a book, though he struggled to retain the verbal information as well. Repetition was important. He often needed to watch TV shows and movies multiple times in order to understand them. Mary and I noticed that he sometimes switched on the closed captioning as well. The words and the sounds evidently reinforced each other and helped him better understand. Very creative! It was amazing to find out how much he simply did not get right away.

We also learned that he had poor planning skills, sometimes known as inferior executive function, meaning that he struggled to link steps together or to connect future consequences to his actions. He could become easily overwhelmed. The "choices" Sergeant Smith told him he had might not have been so clear to him.

The tests showed that basic planning was very difficult for him, which explained Andrew's struggles in basketball lessons at the local YMCA. Unable to grasp the concept of a set play, he would just run up and down the court with the other kids, having no concept of where he was supposed to be. One day on the way home in the car, he confessed that he liked the shooting practice and wind sprints better than playing a game. We stopped going after a while.

It was similar with skateboarding. While Andrew could execute highly difficult tricks in isolation, he was lost in skateboard competitions where one is expected to string together a series of moves. He simply could not plan and execute a coordinated series of moves. After one or two, he got stuck.

The testing was very helpful, both for us as parents and for his teachers. Wainwright tailored some useful changes to Andrew's program. South Orange had tried to do some of the same tests, like the Wechsler Intelligence Test for Children (WISC), but the psychologist, Dr. Zurick, eventually ran out of time and gave up due to Andrew's resistance. We hoped that this new Wainwright knowledge, plus applying new approaches derived from the learning, would help make Andrew feel less frustrated and, in turn, improve his behavior—but after a whole year at Wainwright there was little progress on that front.

Wainwright was very strict on maintaining proper behavior in classes, which was a heavy tax on Andrew's anger and oppositional tendencies. His first year at Wainwright taught us to take things one day at a time. Andrew's misbehavior was demanding increasingly more of my time each week—time that could have gone to building my consulting business or just being with Mary or Margaux.

Wainwright was also very fond of paper. The teachers and experts on staff generated stacks of reports. Andrew's backpack was loaded with announcements and assignments for us and him. Homework had to be signed by the parents. There were extensive rules and protocols that the staff made enormous efforts to maintain.

But I was missing Dr. Ferry, the psychologist. If anything, Andrew was headed in the wrong direction at Wainwright. One year into these weekly sessions, I had a mounting suspicion that Dr. Petrov's primary skill was in feeding the bureaucratic structure. He didn't relate well to Andrew or me, and was at loggerheads with Mary.

Dr. Petrov was obviously frustrated too. The truth that festered underneath every cautious word he and I exchanged that day was that, despite all the attention, resources, new drugs, and expertise, Andrew seemed to be getting worse. We all thought that the school would help him blossom, but instead we just found more weeds.

"He has been seen punching himself in the face and talking to himself," Dr. Petrov continued. "He is embarrassed, ashamed of his behavior, even though he pretends that he's being picked on."

I had a very hard time attending these sessions, but the rules were clear. Someone from the family had to be present. Meanwhile, Andrew was nearby having his "normal" school day. I didn't know how to respond and had to choose my words carefully.

"I'm quite shocked by this comment," I said. "I never got the impression he was ashamed. Maybe embarrassed, from moment to moment, but not ashamed. It's not his fault, after all, that he's sick."

"Yes, and Andrew seems to think that he is entitled to behave as he wishes sometimes," he continued. "Mary has accused us of making a big deal over nothing. You seem to disagree with her, though. Is that right?"

"Yes, I disagree," I said quietly.

I hated being forced to take this position, and sat simmering in Dr. Petrov's windowless office. Little did he know how much I disagreed with Mary on many things. At one point Dr. Ferry had agreed to see Mary and me again as a marriage counselor, but after only one session Mary refused to go back. I was feeling acutely alone across from Dr. Petrov.

Mary had also resisted my assertion that Andrew exhibited a condition we came to call "the lookdown." I sent a description of it to both Mary and the school after sitting down with Andrew to hash out the symptoms.

Andrew Francesco's "The Lookdown" Dystonic Drug Reaction[1]

What it is, how he feels, how he looks, and how you can tell

Optically:
- *Dilated pupils—sensitive to light, can be slight to severe.*
- *Fast fluttering of the eyelids with eyes closed (a key indicator).*

Touching/Tactile:

- *Touching surfaces as if to compare and maybe feel somehow in control of the "fuzzy" feeling in the head.*

Thought Process:

- *He likes to "look down."*
- *Staring at and comparing things that are small in size.*
- *There is a narrowing of focus, mentally, visually, almost as if the lens on a camera closes down in a close-up picture. No TV, for example: the colors are too bright, stories too complex.*
- *Asks people to repeat or explain simple things. Asks questions with obvious answers.*
- *Compulsive thinking of thoughts over and over again. Recurrent fixed ideas and thoughts.*

Emotionally:

- *Does not like to be alone. May follow a trusted person around.*
- *Does not like to lie down in a bed. Prefers sitting quietly and looking down.*
- *Agitation and/or anxiety and nervousness.*
- *Feels very insecure and embarrassed.*
- *Paranoia, feeling that people "are staring at me."*

Appearance:

- *Warm, pink cheeks, possibly from increased blood pressure.*
- *Blunted affect. Face is expressionless and "wooden."*

Triggers:

- *Stress, hunger, and fatigue, perhaps sudden warmth (like in a bath or shower).*

The staff psychiatrist at Wainwright, whom we rarely talked to, eventually added Cogentin—an off-label Parkinson's disease drug—as a supplement to control possible side effects of the antipsychotic Risperdal.

Sitting with Dr. Petrov, my mind flashed back to the huge fight that Mary and I had a week before. I was in the kitchen with my mind on Andrew and Wainwright, reaching for my own blood pressure medicine, when I decided to peek into Andrew's weekly pill dispenser. Andrew was completely off stimulants for the first time since he was eight years old—a nod perhaps to the success of Wainwright's intensive counseling and teaching of coping skills. Per the Wainwright psychiatrist, he was receiving:

DRUG	DOSE	TYPE	NOTES
Risperdal	2 mg in AM and PM	Antipsychotic	Anger control, anxiety
Cogentin	0.5 mg daily	Parkinson's drug	Manages side effects of Risperdal
Luvox	25 mg in AM, 50 mg in PM	Antidepressant	Mood stabilizer
Clonidine	0.1 mg before bed	Blood pressure drug	Sleep inducer

Mary had divvied out his pills for the week, according to the list I kept taped to the cabinet to keep track of changes. But each day had a serious dosage mistake for Andrew's Risperdal.

"Hey," I said when Mary came into the kitchen a few minutes later. "There's a double dose of Risperdal in all the days for Andrew. Do you realize that?"

It was unfortunately easy to make such a mistake, with Andrew's complicated and ever shifting regimen. On top of this, his pills could arrive in different shapes, sizes, and colors, according to availability at the pharmacy.

"Let me see," she said, reaching for the dispenser.

"He's still getting two milligrams of Risperdal twice a day, but they're coming in two-milligram pills now instead of one milligram. Same dose, but the pill changed."

Mary had inadvertently loaded eight milligrams per day instead of four. She was worn down by the routine, but had never made a mistake like this before.

"Oh, well," she said. "I'll fix it. Sorry." She began picking out the extra pills. "I'm just so tired of all of this," she added.

She was burned out and near the end of her rope, taking steady abuse from Andrew at home on top of everything. He was constantly making rude and sexual comments to her, as a new hormone monster was rearing out of control inside him. I was furious over the lack of concern in her voice, though, and we argued.

Mary's behavior overall had started to grow strange, in fact. The stress had been steadily building for both of us, but she sometimes said or did things that made it hard for me to be with her. I wished I could persuade her into serious marital therapy, or even private therapy for herself, but she steadfastly refused. She'd become tired of me, too. She was tired of Andrew's abuse, tired of Wainwright, and just plain tired.

Our kitchen fight got loud and brought in other issues. I'm sure Andrew heard us. That type of fighting was rare for us, and something we'd never let happen in front of the kids. On rare instances in the past, we'd get in the car and drive somewhere to talk, like the South Mountain Reservation. This fight, however, broke out spontaneously. My frustrations finally bubbled over. I was tired of her resistance to Andrew's negative behavior reports from the school, and the medication error set me off. We caught ourselves before long and retreated to separate parts of the house.

"Mary and I are not on the same page these days," I said to Dr. Petrov. "She's grown weary from all the pressure around Andrew. She's also disagreeing with me on Andrew's discipline needs. She's always been afraid that she'll lose his love if she's too tough with him. He tests her very hard sometimes, and she puts up with it."

"Yes?"

"She and I are not consistent with him. I've tried all kinds of ways to reason with her, but she takes her own road. I think kids sometimes need tough love. She seems unwilling to give it, though."

"You two are confusing him, and that carries over to school."

"I know," I said, "but we're not getting anywhere close to getting our differences resolved right now."

"Please understand that, as parents, if you go against the guidance of the school, we can drop Andrew from the program. So you'll need to make more effort to work together with us."

I resented this threat, but I couldn't overlook its gravity, with Andrew's behavior only getting worse. He was supposedly getting the best care possible, but nothing seemed to be getting through, and I didn't know what else to do. Wainwright's connection to Andrew felt distant and bureaucratic. Mary clearly didn't trust Dr. Petrov's judgment and thought he made too big a deal of minor issues. Andrew treated him with barely concealed contempt when we all met together. I was still on the fence about his skills—perhaps unfairly. I questioned what skills or traits led a psychologist into this type of institutional practice. His work role was as much administrator as it was psychologist. With Dr. Ferry's private practice, on the other hand, there was never any doubt about the quality of his engagement and understanding.

"OK," I said to Dr. Petrov. "I promise to talk some more with Mary about his behavior at school."

"So I'll see you *and* Mary next week?" he said.

The unspoken terms were pretty clear. It was now on me to keep Dr. Petrov happy, or Andrew could get kicked out. My head felt like it was stuck in a three-way vice between Wainwright, Mary, and Andrew—with the Aventis situation twisting the screws even harder.

"I'll try," I said. "I'll be here, at least."

While I waited in the hall for Andrew to come out, I felt a wave of depression wash over me. I was caught thinking about the slowdown in my consulting business. My recent efforts with the company were not successful. Before, I could talk to Mary when things got bad, but her depression, fatigue, and volatile reactions now prevented me. The neverending challenges with Andrew had driven a wedge between us as a couple, and had challenged the basic foundation of our marriage.

The unexamined constant in this saga, I now realize, was the medication approach to Andrew's problems—over five years, three schools, and multiple doctors and counselors. The ceremony of writing and passing over each new prescription had taken on an almost religious quality. Each new diagnosis and alteration to Andrew's prescriptions was delivered like a fresh revelation. Leaving the office each time, we felt that we had been absolved of our sins and blessed, yet Andrew never ended up any closer to redemption.

The medication management ritual assumed that drugs were helping, or at least that the next drug might help, always reaching toward a chemical solution. Why is this approach so unquestioned? One could reasonably take another point of view: that increasing chemical dependence without signs of improvement could be called an unhealthy forced addiction for the taker—and, for the prescriber, critically poor judgment, or an ongoing delusion that he is doing something to improve the patient's health. It can become a circle of the absurd, each party hoping for a positive result but all based on wrong assumptions. The key sacrament in this relationship was the drugs. We were all caught in worship of a false god: better health through chemistry!

Andrew's schools and doctors pushed us to medicate. But why, after so many years, and so many diagnoses and prescriptions, had we seen no discernible improvement? If anything, Andrew's struggles had gotten worse in concert with his increased intake of and dependence on the drugs. Still, the doctors were willing to add more. I was confused and uncomfortable with his frequently shifting diagnoses, some of which seemed like results rather than causes of medication changes. Was the real sin that we continued to medicate? Was the psychiatrist more like a shaman leading us astray? Was the children's mental health tribe (the drug makers, insurance companies, doctors, and scholastic institutions) covertly pushing us past the point of redemption?

"Hey, Big Guy. How was your day?" I said when Andrew found me in the hallway.

"It sucked. Like usual."

"No lookdown?" I asked.

"Nope. Just the usual sucky day."

We walked the rest of the way to the car without talking.

"Are we still going to the mall?" he asked while climbing in.

I'd promised to take him on the way home. Maybe if I bought him something, I thought, I could use his elevated mood to get him to open up. Andrew had become obsessed with malls and always needed to buy something new. He'd really taken the bait of the product marketers—the familiar belief that some new item will make you happier—but I was willing to play along for a time.

He was resistant to talk, Mary was resistant to talk, and there was tremendous tension between them. Andrew continued to make inappropriate sexual comments to Mary, and Wainwright's reports confirmed his onslaught of sexual thoughts. So why did Mary tell the school that they were making a big deal out of nothing?

We stopped at GameStop, Andrew's favorite destination. I didn't know how else to get him engaged. He wanted an expensive new-release game and replacement headset. He'd become more and more demanding; Dr. Ferry once told us that this behavior was an attempt to fill a void, an empty feeling inside him. However, as soon as Andrew had the game and headset back in the car, he was struck with buyer's remorse[2] and wanted to replace the headset.

Knowing that his reaction to any other item would be just the same, I refused. I tried to reason with him, pleading with him to try the headset and then return it if he wanted. It was frustrating to feel like I was throwing money away like this, given the insecurity around my business, but I didn't know what else to do. It was critical that I find a way to open him up; it wasn't happening at Wainwright.

Instead of getting him to talk about his feelings or his relationship with Mary, though, our argument in the car just ratcheted up higher. We fought most of the way home. There was a one-mile section of South Orange Avenue that I came to call the Battle Zone, where this scenario had played out multiple times.

By the time we got into our driveway, I was already yearning for the first taste of scotch. There would be more than one.

CHAPTER EIGHT

Then Thunder

June 2007

That winter brought more lightning strikes to illuminate and inflame the crisis around Andrew. Then, in June, two enormous and gut-wrenching thunderclaps sent the Francesco family spinning fully out of control.

The first: Andrew was not allowed to continue at Wainwright.

The separation document, which profiled him and was to be sent to other potential schools, was simply brutal. His diagnoses had expanded. According to the document, he suffered from the following, in order:

1. *Bipolar, Not Otherwise Specified*
2. *Tourette's Disorder*
3. *Obsessive-Compulsive Disorder*
4. *Oppositional Defiant Disorder*

The version of Andrew Dr. Petrov described in the document was not the troubled child I had watched struggle with an unenviable set of mental challenges. Dr. Petrov's comments castigated Andrew as a mean-spirited and deliberately misbehaving teenager. At the separation meeting, attended by myself, the Wainwright headmaster, Dr. Petrov, and a representative from the South Orange school system, I could hardly contain my fury.

"Andrew wouldn't even be allowed into a reform school with this document!" I said with as much calm as I could muster. "What a terrible thing to have written down formally and follow him in his file to the next school!"

I turned to the neutral representative from South Orange. "Have you ever seen such a scandalous description of a fourteen-year-old?"

"No," she replied. "It's shocking in its negativity to this child."

"This is a disgrace," I said. "It has to be redone and significantly moderated."

"We do not revise our termination documents here at Wainwright," Dr. Petrov quickly interjected with an air of papal infallibility.

The headmaster remained silent.

"Who is the shrink for the shrink?" I appealed to him, mockingly. "This document tells more about a lack of balance and understanding on the part of the author than it does about the patient."

But the institution had spoken. Andrew was turned away with

nothing to recommend him but a modified drug regimen, this time with increased Risperdal:

DRUG	DOSE	TYPE	NOTES
Risperdal	3 mg in AM / 2 mg in PM	Antipsychotic	Anger control, anxiety
Cogentin	0.5 mg daily	Parkinson's drug	Manages side effects of Risperdal
Luvox	25 mg in AM, 50 mg in PM	Antidepressant	Mood stabilizer

The termination document additionally stated that "until the parents make Andrew take responsibility for his actions, the prognosis is guarded for his improvement."

I left that part alone. It may have been true.

The search was back on for a new school, and it was time to call Mrs. Lynch again. This time, due to the nasty separation document, we would have to include schools where Andrew could live full-time and get closer attention, as a new option. We were getting pushed further away from any vision of normalcy.

Then, the second blast of thunder: Mary was diagnosed with her second bout of breast cancer. We had been through her first bout nine years earlier and she had been getting follow-up exams and taking tamoxifen as a deterrent.

When she was diagnosed, we were living apart in a trial separation. Despite the pain and loneliness of our failing marriage, living apart had brought us a degree of relief. Both of our lives were simplified, with Mary insulated from Andrew and with Mary and I insulated from each other.

Mary bravely pressed on. We worked together to find another school for Andrew, and the new challenges helped force a reconciliation between us. Our hostilities fizzled out around the larger priorities of her recuperation and Andrew's next school. I picked her up and shuttled her around for food shopping and doctor visits. The separate living seemed to be helping everybody. Margaux magnificently and lovingly decided to take a year off of college to live with Mary and help her in anything she needed. They became even closer.

I had a much simpler life being responsible for only Andrew and myself. I was even seeing hints of improvement in my consulting business. Yet I couldn't escape the feeling that Mary was emotionally drifting away from me, and it broke my heart.

How I wish things came out differently. The family I worked so hard to build was shattered. The keys to which I had committed my life were career, family, love, and good quality of life—but everything seemed destroyed.

It was overwhelming. I felt equally helpless against Mary's cancer and Andrew's mental ailments. Although I could maintain the ability to function, I felt hollow inside. There were the desperate drives to Susan's chemotherapy, seeing her weaken gradually. We would talk normally but this was all a front. I also had the question of whether we would ever find a new school for Andrew. He also had a hard time accepting her hampered walk. I never drove her with Andrew in the car now.

For both Mary and Andrew, the pharmaceutical industry was waiting with a heavily marketed narrative of hope and relief. Our family was unforeseeably deep in the clutches of the health care industry—Mary receiving steady medications by pill and injection along with her physical and occupational therapy, and Andrew's unbroken regimen of psychiatric drugs with additional drugs to battle their side effects. I estimated the monthly charges to our insurer were upwards of $12,000, and we were extremely lucky to have these options available to us. I had been paying for this expensive health care policy for a long time, and it was covering me through the terrible crisis, thank God.

Johnnie Walker was not covered under our policy, but I relied on it heavily during this time. I reflected on how little we are able to control in our lives, how little we understand the roots of many common conditions, and, in the case of Andrew, how random and ineffective the medication approach can be for fighting them.

We've truly become a society of drug takers. Everyone—in business and in practice—buys into the notion that, given a problem, there is probably a pill for it. This was far from true for both Mary and Andrew. Still, in times of overwhelming desperation, it is very easy to suspend judgment. It is very easy to accept the well-established and expensively marketed narrative that some drug will hold the answer. With Andrew, could the drugs have actually been part of the problem? When the drugs miss their purported target, they must land somewhere in the body.

Was there no alternative?

CHAPTER NINE

Only Hope Remains

January 2008

The separate living situation left a lot of new time for Andrew and me to spend guy-to-guy. Andrew was still in between schools, and we were sitting in Taco Bell in Milburn, New Jersey, just killing time one afternoon when he looked over to me. He'd been staring at another table filled with boys around his age, all laughing, eating tacos, and sharing inside jokes. There was a note of sadness I'd never heard before in his voice when he said, "I wish I could be like them."

Andrew was fourteen years old. I'd hired a tutor for him during the fall semester, as we continued searching for a new school to accept him.

A deep mix of optimism, shame, and yearning welled in him. I was trying to keep him as content as I could under the circumstances, sitting together in the fast food restaurant. I recognized the underlying and familiar questions that bucked in his young brain. *Will I ever have friends of my own? Why is something always wrong with me?*

Since he was three years old, Andrew had lived with mental or neurological health issues. Depending on the year, the doctor, and the school, he had been diagnosed with obsessive-compulsive disorder, Tourette's disorder, oppositional defiant disorder, bipolar disorder, attention deficit hyperactivity disorder, and more. The adults and experts attached these names, but to him it was just the challenge of everyday life.

His misbehavior was an unending battle. No one outside the family could fully appreciate how much and how bravely he had suffered in the past eleven years. Over that time, in our desperation, we'd overseen him on more than twenty different prescription medications. None of them were the key to a happy, safe, and adjusted childhood. It was certainly not for lack of trying.

"Friends aren't such a big deal," I said. "Look at me. I didn't have very many friends when I was your age. It took time to find the right people as I got older."

"I wish I could be like them," he repeated.

"It's OK, Big Guy. Once we get you into a new school, you'll make plenty of friends. I promise. We just haven't found it yet."

As his father, times like these were rare and valuable. Before Taco Bell, we had gone to the Short Hills Mall. Andrew had new yellow-orange hair that Mary had helped him color, and he skated around the gleaming floors on his sneakers with built-in wheels. He skated beautifully and was trying so hard to have fun, but he was the only non-adult in the whole mall. It was early afternoon on a school day, and the fluorescent-lit and vaulted mall ceilings echoed with the absence of other people his age.

Andrew looked at me again after my little friendship speech. We'd been at this long enough that he didn't need words to say, *Thanks, Dad. I know what you're doing, but it's not OK. I know that I'm the problem, and I'm sorry. I keep hoping that things will change. I promise to keep trying.*

He went back to playing with the taco sauce packets. As his father, I was most responsible for helping Andrew find improvement. Was the next school, the next set of medications, or the next doctor going to provide that elusive combination to get us out of his cycle of frustration and disappointment?

As an entrepreneur in the health care industry, certain skills led directly to my success: keen judgment and analysis, creative recognition of opportunities, and productive team building. With Andrew, however, my best efforts had only taken us in circles. And the very best combined efforts from the children's mental health industry had brought us here: father and son, sitting alone on a school day afternoon at Taco Bell. Whatever was going on with Andrew had yet to be cracked, and there was little indication that the situation would change.

Watching the other boys in Taco Bell, I found myself entertaining the same hope as Andrew—for a miracle. There were no better visible options. And a miracle would not have been our first with regard to Andrew.

Before Mary became pregnant with Andrew, we'd given up hope of having a second child. Margaux was born in 1988, and after trying for a sibling for several years, we were ready to give up. As a final effort, we consulted with a well-known fertility doctor. He examined Mary and me, ran some tests, and provided some medication, but concluded that Mary was highly unlikely to conceive again. We'd resigned ourselves to this fate when Mary came out of the bathroom one morning in January 1993.

"I think I'm pregnant," she said.

She immediately went out to our local drugstore in South Orange and bought three different pregnancy tests. All three confirmed her feeling—a miracle. Andrew was born healthy and normal, except for the rare presence of a single baby tooth.[1] It was a portent that he would be special.

In retrospect, did we make a mistake by not treating his strange spells as a toddler? As a health care consultant, I was in an improved position to seek additional information. I should have pursued a second (and third) opinion. Working closely with doctors, I know that they are only human and often rely on limited prior experience to make decisions. Looking back, I wish that we had tapped into my professional network to get more information. Maybe some intervention could have altered the course of Andrew's life. What if one drug back then could have saved him the twenty later? What if the problem could have been addressed without any drugs in the first place?

Our parental instincts at the time, though, appeared to be correct. Andrew came through the woods and appeared to develop normally. And, sitting in Taco Bell, I could only hope for similar grace.

CHAPTER TEN

Back on the Beach at Rockport

Rockport, Massachusetts
August 20, 2008

From my chair on the familiar sand of Rockport Beach, I watched Andrew dip in and out of the crashing waves. I wanted to get away for a week to decompress and to give Andrew some time outdoors, in his element. His body had grown a lot in the previous year. He looked much closer to a man now than a child, as he faced off against the rolling breakers. Body surfing now, at his new size, he could really stretch out and get a good long ride.

The sun sat high and still in the sky, covering the beach in baking heat. I'd hoped to find some peace and echoes of past comfort by returning to Rockport, but it was wishful thinking. The familiar space only reminded me of what was different.

Mary had passed away in April from her cancer. At least she had peace now. Neighbors put together a wonderful memorial service. Mary was loved. I had been with her for twenty-four years. Here at the beach I felt conspicuously alone. The memories that sprang up only seemed to amplify the void she left behind. I tried to read or just soak in the sun, but my attention was pulled back again and again to the empty sand beside me where Mary's chair should have been.

Her decline was quick and, I'm convinced, intricately related to the stress of raising Andrew. She was worn down and kept constantly on edge. Her spirit had leaked away. Stress is proven to reduce the body's natural immune defenses,[1] and spiritual depletion opens the door for sickness even wider. I missed Mary tremendously. I had vivid and visceral memories from our last trip to Rockport, when we were all a family in a quest for some small sense of normalcy. Normalcy was an even bigger challenge now, and one that I faced alone.

I was extra thankful for Margaux, for her loving support of Mary up to the very end. I was thankful that she was able to live a healthy and independent young-adult life. After all the pressures she faced from her role in the family, I was relieved to see her begin to move on. She was looking at colleges again for her sophomore year. Margaux had declined to join Andrew and me for this trip. She was busy and probably knew it would remind her too strongly of her mother's absence. In retrospect, it may have been the wiser choice.

Mary fought so bravely through her depleted energy, intense pain and discomfort. When we were together she insisted that I maintain a positive attitude around the kids, never treating her ordeal as an incurable death sentence. I admired her strength.

I'll never forget the look she gave me when she announced to us that she had just heard the cancer diagnosis. We hadn't been face-to-face for several days. In one hot, split second her eyes told me: *Steve, don't you dare alarm the kids. I know how serious this is, and I am going to handle it in my own way. I want you to keep this as positive as absolutely as possible.*

And with all of her strength, she did. She continued to be a supportive parent. Andrew had a failed placement at a fourth out-of-district school in September, and Mary insisted on accompanying me to the school meetings, despite her limited mobility.

I was caught deep in this mournful reflection when Andrew dropped down in the sand beside me, like old times. His love for the place was thankfully undiminished, and that managed to lift my spirits. He was so fully at home on that beach, so in the moment. He burrowed himself into the sand, digging in with his newly wide shoulders. He flipped sand onto his stomach and chest, wrapping himself in it.

In two days he would be fifteen, and I wondered what kind of adult might be able to grow from his checkered and difficult childhood. Though Mary's death still weighed heavily on the family, I could see glimmers of a new confidence and presence in him. He'd recently begun a summer program at his fifth out-of-district school. The Clarion School was a subsidiary to a well-established mental health facility. They had agreed to take Andrew for the summer as a trial to see if he might be able to continue there in the fall.

So far, I was cautiously optimistic that we wouldn't be back on another new school search come September. This trip was an opportunity for us to be together, and I hoped it might help him with a boost of self-esteem. I hoped also that it would be a chance for us to bond as father and son, to provide a stronger foundation in case I had to come down on him about his behavior at the new school.

After a while Andrew rose up, the sand cascading off him, and dug into the bag of sandwiches we'd brought from the deli.

"You hungry, Dad?"

"Sure, Big Guy. Thanks."

He passed me my turkey sandwich and tore into his chicken parm. All around us other families were doing what families do—they ate and talked, and the kids played together in the sand and the shallow water. We sat and ate together, just listening to the sound of waves heaving onto the beach. I was comforted in a small way that Mary and I had stayed connected, in our way, through to the end. I'd heard that divorce rates were pretty high for parents of children with special needs; thank God we never got there.

Andrew and I had actually grown closer after her death. It was perhaps a result of his new dependence on me as a single parent. We uncovered new ways to communicate, often without speaking. Sitting on the beach together, amid all the action, his expression said it all: *I'm still here, Dad.*

We continued eating and listening to the waves.

"Hey, Big Guy," I said between bites. "Why'd the chicken cross the road?" A silly dad line to break our silence.

"Cause he had a date on the other side," he replied, right on beat. "Probably some hot chick."

The Andrew I saw at the beach buoyed my hope that he could find success at this new school in the fall. If only there was a way to translate the calmness he showed there on the beach into regular life.

That night, Andrew and I were in the quiet kitchen of our rental house, feeling relaxed and tired out from our day in the sun. We were just milling around, with the TV playing a ballgame in the other room, getting ready to eventually head out for a pizza dinner.

"You ready for pizza?" I said.

"Dad. When am I not ready for pizza?"

Something about dinner reminded me strongly of Mary's loss, of our last Rockport dinner together in the kitchen of our rental house, three years before. I looked at Andrew, trying to hide my emotion. Then, overcome, I threw my arms around him and hugged him hard. He put his now manly arms over my shoulders and hugged me back. We cried together next to the kitchen table, sharing our feelings again wordlessly. It was like we were the only two people on earth, father and son.

I miss her.

So do I, Dad. And I'm sorry.

Why did you have to treat her like you did?

I didn't know how to react.

It's OK. You were just a kid.

I'm sorry.

So am I.

I wish that I could show her somehow.

It was amazing how much Mary gave. She was so depressed and so diligent for so long. The rest of the night, it felt like her old spirit, from before any of our troubles, was there with us. It lingered in our rental house for the rest of the week. We didn't talk about her, but she was a silent part of everything we did and said.

Before we drove back to New Jersey, I'd arranged a fifteenth birthday celebration for Andrew at my sister's house. Though situations like these could be tense with Andrew's behavior, my sister and her son were very loving and supportive. She made a wonderful meal and birthday cake for the occasion. I hoped that Andrew's recent progress with self-esteem would make for a smooth night. Astonishingly, my hopes were rewarded, and then some. The Andrew who came through the door of my sister's house was almost unrecognizable.

"OK, are you ready for three balls?" he said, from his make-shift stage on the living room carpet. "You start off with two, one in each hand, before you add the third. First, toss the ball from your right hand, in an arc to about eye level, over to your left hand, like this."

Andrew stood steadily before my sister and her son, giving a juggling demonstration. As soon as we arrived, in fact, he had started putting on a show. It was remarkable. He was confidant, articulate, and totally charming—like he had grown years in a week's vacation.

"When this ball reaches the highest point in the arc, throw the ball in your left hand in an arc to your right, like this. Then do that a bunch of times to get comfortable with the toss and catch."

We all watched smiling.

"Now you add the third ball."

The black and grey juggling balls went flying gracefully through the air in perfect arcs. Andrew received and re-launched each one in a smooth rhythm. He looked so comfortable. It was like he'd been doing it his whole life. I knew that he'd taken to the juggling class I found for him a few months before, but his poise and clear communication while he juggled was stunning. He quickly caught the balls and placed them down on the table, a genuine smile on his face.

The Clarion School had reported to me before vacation that Andrew seemed to be undergoing a breakthrough in his social interaction. I wondered if maybe I was witnessing it. Andrew's joyful performance cast a happy glow that began the evening. He was relaxed, intelligent, and funny throughout. For years Andrew had struggled in situations like these.

The Clarion School employed a range of alternative therapeutic approaches, different from anything we'd tried before with Andrew. One of these involved a special therapy dog named Beauty. Clarion informed me that Andrew had developed a strong attachment to the dog. Whenever Andrew got angry, Beauty would back away from him—a simple and intuitive consequence for his behavior. And with Beauty's presence at stake, he'd begun to learn better control of his emotions. The basic, immediate feedback from Beauty was evidently helping him learn to link consequences to his actions and rein in his behavior accordingly.

The entirety of Andrew's birthday dinner was lovely. At the end of the evening, Andrew stood in front of everyone again. "This has been a perfect birthday dinner in every way," he said, fully commanding his nearly grown-up body. "Thank you very much."

He'd planned this whole little routine, as maybe he did the juggling show. He was scoring points with his speaking and performing. My sister beamed.

On our drive back to New Jersey, we talked the whole way—some of the best talking we'd ever done. He opened up about his excitements and fears for the new school. I was even optimistic about Andrew's medication for the first time in many years.

We had a new psychiatrist on the case who'd made major changes to Andrew's diagnosis and treatment strategy. Dr. Bainer had concluded that Andrew did not actually show evidence of an affective disorder like depression or bipolar. He narrowed the diagnosis to Tourette's disorder with accompanying attention deficit hyperactivity disorder and obsessive-compulsive disorder. Tourette's is considered a neurological disorder rather than an emotional disorder, which is a critical distinction.

After this new diagnosis, we gradually took Andrew off of Depakote, Risperdal, Luvox, and clonidine. Dr. Bainer prescribed him a new cocktail of lithium, Luvox, and Seroquel:

DRUG	DOSE	TYPE	NOTES
Lithium	600 mg twice per day	Antipsychotic	Regular blood tests required to monitor dosage
Luvox	200 mg at night	SSRI	Mood stabilizer
Seroquel	200 mg AM and PM	Second-generation atypical antipsychotic	Needed to control anger

The standard medication management approach, as ever, would monitor for any potential problems from these new drugs. *Was this new medication finally helping Andrew make progress?* Perhaps Dr. Bainer was finally closing in on the root of his struggles.

That summer day in 2008 on our drive back to New Jersey, it seemed that the elements were actually aligning—the early stages of a profound change. Finally, God was in heaven and things were right in the world with regard to Andrew. I only wished that Mary could have been there to share it.

CHAPTER ELEVEN

Redemption

2008-2009
October 17, 2008, 2 PM

Thanks to Andrew's progress, he was invited for the fall term at The Clarion School. A month in, my hopes from the summer were being remarkably fulfilled.

"It looks like we may be on a good streak," Ms. Faith told me privately in a counseling room at Clarion after a session with Andrew. "But don't forget that things can change quickly. It's good to stay hopeful, but realistic."

Ms. Faith was Andrew's chief counselor and had invited me to join her session with Andrew that day. She was a certified clinical social worker and exceptionally kind, warm, and patient. She managed to get into Andrew's psyche in a way that no one else was able to.

For the meeting, Andrew sat on a chair next to Beauty. Beauty was a regal-looking border collie with a shiny black and white coat. I sat on the floor out of the way and was instructed to stay quiet unless addressed by Ms. Faith. There was something noticeably different in the air at The Clarion School. It was founded in 1920, interestingly, well before the explosive trend of reactive psychopharmacology. A lot of Clarion's practices could be traced back to more classical methods, and, unlike Andrew's other schools, they left the choice of pharmacologic intervention completely to the parents.

Ms. Faith and Andrew began by talking about a confrontation he'd had in gym class. It was the type of incident that in the past would have ended in a trip for me to pick up Andrew early from school. Ms. Faith calmly took him back through it. Andrew was engaged and clearly proud to report how he had been able to control his anger. Throughout his story, Beauty sat right at his side.

I could barely contain my excitement from where I sat in the corner. It was like watching a different person. The darkness and anger that so often seemed to overwhelm Andrew never appeared.

"Andrew," Ms. Faith interrupted, "do you see that Beauty hasn't moved once since we started talking?"

Andrew looked over happily at Beauty.

"Does that make you feel good?"

"Yes."

The meeting went on like this. I could barely contain my excitement in the corner. I wanted to jump up and hug him. I wanted to buy him every game in GameStop.

So much about The Clarion School broke from what had become our "normal" relationships with Andrew's schools. It felt like they were finally getting through. We were working together as a team, with actual visible results, rather than dancing delicately around a raw situation. I was amazed to see the powerful effect that Beauty was having on Andrew close up. I'd heard of therapy horses before, but never therapy dogs.[1] The deep-hitting intuitive behavioral lessons he got from the dog simply blew away the many years' worth of other tactics. He was able to translate and apply these lessons in his relations with people as well.

"He's been doing very well," continued Ms. Faith in our private meeting. "Andrew has made some important changes to his way of thinking. He's now able to recognize his impulsivity and let the moment pass. It's resulted in him having far less conflict during the day. He's been showing some very positive results in his relations with his peers as well. "

"Ms. Faith, you're doing an amazing job," I said.

I was looking hard at the floor, trying to hold back my emotions. I knew that just seeing her exceptionally warm and bright, professionally collected face could make me burst. Ever since Mary passed away, things as simple as a falling leaf could trigger a river of burning tears. I'd become unfortunately expert at choking back my sadness. People had told me that the effort showed on my face, even though I didn't make a sound.

"Well, thank you," she said. "Andrew deserves most of the credit. He's been making great strides. He's working independently now on the computer and relating constructively with his classmates. We're discussing moving him up a grade in math."

What a change from the previous June. The Andrew who first appeared at Clarion was a long shot to even be invited for the fall semester.

I twisted my left foot into the floor, trying to find a valve that wouldn't leave me sobbing in front of Ms. Faith.

"He just seems so much more grounded and confident," I said. "He's doing really well at home, too."

My eyes were welling. Eventually a few drops fell out. I excused myself and went to the nearby staff men's room. My body was almost shaking. Everything that had built up for the last year—Mary, Andrew, the doubts, the struggles, the fear of failure, the hints at success—seemed to hit me all once. I let myself cry in the stall for about thirty seconds. "Control yourself, Steve." I quickly wiped away the tears and took a deep breath, exhaling slowly before I rejoined Ms. Faith.

Ms. Faith kept her poise and gave just a hint of a professional, approving smile.

"We'll do our best to keep on this track," she said. "Fingers crossed. I have to get on to my next student now. Please do feel free to call me tomorrow if you'd like to talk further."

After a string of frustration and sadness that spanned more than half of Andrew's life, it really seemed like we had turned a corner.

"Thanks again," I managed to say as she went out.

We'd put in so much effort before without seeing any progress. What accounted for this change? Ms. Faith's approach with Andrew was very different from that of Dr. Petrov at the Wainwright Academy. She was kind, thoughtful, and did not take a chastising angle with him. The school employed a therapeutic approach that was evolved and institutionalized well before the trend to reflexively or defensively turn to medication in the 1980s. The Clarion School kept no medical doctors on staff, though the school nurse was available to dispense medications during the school day, fully at the discretion of each family and the family's self-selected doctors.

We continued to meet with Dr. Bainer. In the fall Dr. Bainer added back the secondary diagnosis of *emerging bipolar disorder* to Andrew's sheet and increased his dose of Seroquel. In my experience, the bipolar label seemed to function as a sort of catch-all diagnosis that allowed doctors more leeway to pursue the medication approach. I continued to doubt its veracity, but the results were, for the first time, compelling. I didn't want to rock the boat.

Andrew's Seroquel dose was quite heavy, more than the recommended dosage for an adult, but Dr. Bainer assured me that this second-generation atypical antipsychotic was very safe and was helping Andrew to manage his anger and impulsivity.

DRUG	DOSE	TYPE	NOTES
Lithium	600 mg twice per day	Mood stabilizer	Regular blood tests required to monitor dosage
Luvox	200 mg at night	SSRI	Mood stabilizer
Seroquel	400 mg AM and PM with 100 mg extra at 11 AM at school	Second-generation atypical antipsychotic	Needed to control anger and impulsivity

Dr. Bainer struck me as an exceptionally kind and professional resource. We had begun seeing him when he was the staff psychiatrist at Andrew's fourth out-of-district school, and decided to continue on after as part of his private practice.

A few months after meeting Andrew, Dr. Bainer became concerned that the heavy volume of medication Andrew was taking was yielding so little relief. Dr. Bainer felt that sharpening his diagnosis was key to effective treatment, and had taken a strong initiative. He'd arranged for a second opinion from another very senior psychiatrist, which led to Andrew's new diagnosis. The result was a much simpler daily schedule of medications and dosages, which included the major addition of lithium, a very old and well-studied mood stabilizer.

Had the combined push from drug companies, doctors, schools, and insurers to feed Andrew a steady and shifting stream of psychiatric medications from such a young age finally paid off with this program? Perhaps we had been right to trust. After six years of attempts, Andrew finally seemed to be on track. It was an almost unbearably long but maybe ultimately gratifying process of trial and error for a difficult, evolving, and complex situation. In retrospect, what alternative did we really have?

As opposed to the immediate and visible influence of one therapy dog, Andrew had trustingly consumed an extensive range of potent medications with negative, inconclusive, or, at best, questionably positive effects for most of his life. Here is the compiled list:

CLASS OF DRUG	DRUG	ANDREW'S AGE	ANDREW'S DIAGNOSES
Stimulant	Ritalin	6	ADHD
Stimulant	Adderall	7	ADHD
Stimulant	Concerta	8, 11	ADHD
Stimulant	Strattera	8	ADHD
Anti-hypertensive	Catapres	7–10, 12	ADHD, bipolar possible
Antidepressant	Zoloft	10	Bipolar—Not Otherwise Specified (NOS)
Anti-convulsant	Trileptal	10–11	Bipolar NOS, ADHD, ODD, OCD
Atypical antipsychotic	Risperdal	11–14	Bipolar NOS, ADHD, ODD, OCD
Antidepressant	Luvox	11–15	Bipolar NOS, ADHD, ODD, OCD

CLASS OF DRUG	DRUG	ANDREW'S AGE	ANDREW'S DIAGNOSES
Anti-Parkinson's disease	Cogentin	12–14	Bipolar NOS, ADHD, ODD, OCD
Anti-hypertensive	Clonidine	12–13	Bipolar NOS, ADHD, ODD, OCD
Antipsychotic	Lithium	14–15	Tourette's disorder, OCD, possible bipolar
Atypical antipsychotic	Seroquel	14–15	Tourette's disorder, OCD, possible bipolar

The Clarion School attitude was a great relief to me. It gave time to pursue the proper diagnoses, techniques, and relationships. I believe that their non-drug-oriented approach and their well-established programs and expertise were the key to the combination of interventions that finally seemed to have Andrew on a positive track.

His progress there continued into the winter, an unseasonably warm one. So much had changed in our lives over the past year that a bizarre winter heat wave only seemed appropriate. The Francesco family searched for its new normal, and I was, for the first time in much longer than I could remember, steadily hopeful for the future. Ms. Faith, Beauty, the rest of The Clarion School, Dr. Bainer, and Dr. Ferry—"Team Andrew"—were solidly in place. The new drug regimen was proving effective, though I still worried about the side effects.

Winter vacation arrived, and Margaux was off from college for Christmas break. We decided not to hang any stockings that year, our first Christmas without Mary. We made our way delicately through some of the holiday traditions, but there was a lot of adjusting still to do. We watched television together late into the night, Andrew, Margaux, and me, together around the sofa as a family. The pain of Mary's absence stood in strange concert with the comfort of Andrew's progress.

Amazingly, Andrew was looking forward to school starting again in January. He missed his classmates. His missed Beauty and his days at Clarion. For the first time in his life, he felt like "one of them."

CHAPTER TWELVE

Interrupted

January 18, 2009, 7:30 AM

"Andrew, let them put on the mask. Let them put it on," I pleaded in the back of the ambulance as we floated over the familiar twists and turns of South Orange Avenue.

The siren blared over the voices of other men in the ambulance, volunteers from our town, all trying to get my son to accept the oxygen mask. I grabbed hold of a wall as the engine whined louder and we rocked and lurched up a twisting hill. The ambulance made a sudden right, and we were on Old Short Hills Road, almost at the St. Barnabas Hospital emergency room.

My son was pale white and gasping for air, unable to speak

and resisting every effort they made to place a mask over his nose and mouth. He was fighting courageously, as if for his life, but his mind was telling him the wrong things.

The day before, a Saturday, Andrew had acted withdrawn. He wouldn't eat or drink. He refused to be touched and had wanted only to lay on his back and watch TV. He'd had a bad cold on Friday night, and I figured that his body was recuperating.

"Andrew, listen to me!" I shouted. "Let them put on the mask! They want to help!"

He was strapped down, but still managed to get his arms free and resist the mask. The EMS crew had hastily wrapped him in white paper. When I'd gone to check on Andrew in his bed that morning, he was lying in feces. I hoped that he was alert enough to recognize my voice over the commotion in the ambulance.

Andrew had been having the best six months of his life. I thought we'd finally broken through. In retrospect, there were warning signs that perhaps I should have pursued more strongly. As a compromise to his improvements at The Clarion School, Andrew had begun to suffer from attacks of twitching and occasional painful headaches.

I raised these issues with Dr. Bainer in our medication management session for December. Our sessions lasted a full hour, in contrast to the production-line style we'd grown accustomed to with other doctors. I would go in first to discuss my concerns for Andrew, then Andrew would go in alone for a chat with the doctor, and the session would end with all of three of us together. Dr. Bainer was not covered by my insurance, but I happily wrote a check on the spot each visit. With his wise and open demeanor, he seemed worth every penny. He was just like the serene, graying, mid-to-late career psychiatrist that you'd expect to see in a movie.

"Andrew, listen to me!" I yelled. "Andrew! Andrew!"

Andrew had grown so much in the last year that he was capably fighting off several grown men. He wheezed for breath while he battled, his skin slowly shifting to a sickly pale blue.

It happened so quickly. Andrew had just finished a busy and positive week. After some debate, I let him go to school on Friday with a cold coming on, instead of staying home and resting. Clarion showed a movie on Fridays as a reward for students who displayed good behavior during the week, and Andrew loved being part of this group. It was a proud and concrete marker for his overall improvement.

The changes in Andrew's behavior were astounding. I was reluctant to do anything that might change his course. Still, I was concerned over what appeared to be side effects, so I pressed Dr. Bainer.

"There are no side effects," said Dr. Bainer in our December meeting.

His desk was strewn with prescription pads and colorful pens given away by pharmaceutical marketers.

"Seroquel has *no* side effects?"

"It's a very safe drug. That's why we chose to go to it, remember?"

In June, when we put together Andrew's new drug schedule, Dr. Bainer had verbally listed the drugs he would consider to go with lithium and Luvox. He was steady in his opinion that Seroquel was the superior choice, and that it was effective in helping Andrew to control his anger. I had no evidence to the contrary.

The Clarion School advised that Andrew see a neurologist to address his twitching and headaches, and I needed a referral from Dr. Bainer.

"I'll refer you to a neurologist, but let's stay with what we've been doing since July for the dosage. From everything you're telling me, he's doing quite well now."

Dr. Bainer scribbled the note into Andrew's file. To complement his calming pace and style, he didn't use a computer. He'd earned my trust as the architect of Andrew's new medication regimen. It can be so hard to read positive effects inside the brain, or what might be causing them, chemically speaking. Side effects like twitching and headaches are easier to note. Andrew was clearly showing major improvements, though. He'd taken a constantly shifting combination of drugs for over half his life, without ever reaching a successful outcome. Each time that Andrew had failed to show definitive improvement, it was the same routine: *try a different medication.* Or, this time with hints of actual improvement, *try more.*

The results from Andrew's visit to the neurologist were inconclusive. I was worried that his intermittent headaches continued, but overall he seemed well. For six months, since he started at Clarion, I'd seen real and dramatic improvement. He was getting things that weren't possible before. We were connecting better person-to-person. There was something newly sturdy behind his eyes, and we'd begun to approach life as a team, with new confidence that things were going to work out.

The ambulance pulled into the emergency room bay at St. Barnabas Hospital. The ride seemed to pass in an unreal state of suspended time. Inside the building things became faster and chaotic. There was a flurry of people, loud sounds, strange smells, flashing lights, and swinging doors. It was like a bad dream.

Andrew was taken into an ER examination room, where he was strapped down to a bed. They attached a heart monitor that was beeping rapidly. Andrew was still struggling against the new team of people trying to keep on the oxygen mask. He was surrounded by emergency personnel, blocking my view. At some point Andrew's pediatrician was standing beside me. I'd had the presence of mind to call him and Dr. Bainer while we waited for

EMS to arrive. Knowing Andrew's case, I thought they might be able to provide input. Children like Andrew can sometimes react strangely to viruses or infection. Our pediatrician had known Andrew all his life and promptly appeared at the hospital.[1] I could see only glimpses of Andrew squirming on the bed.

In the continuing battle to keep the mask on, it was decided to give a shot to immobilize him. Andrew stopped moving instantly, and the heart monitor gave out a steady high-pitched whine: Andrew had flatlined. Everybody in the room stiffened. I watched all this from near the foot of the bed, curiously unfeeling, in shock, trying to process what was happening.

A doctor called out "clear" and placed paddles to Andrew's chest. There was no motion, no life-affirming beep. They jolted him several more times. There was more and sudden frantic motion, and I suddenly found myself outside the room. The pediatrician had guided me out, repeating, "You don't want to see this." The team was inserting an artificial heart stimulator under the skin and performing a tracheotomy to keep his body oxygenated.

Andrew was moved from emergency to the ICU. We'd somehow moved up to the fourth floor when Margaux arrived and met me in the hall. Margaux and I stayed close outside Andrew's room, monitoring the activity.

Initially, the doctors seemed strangely concerned that he could be infectious. Eventually, however, there was a burst of questions regarding Seroquel. I told them that I was in charge of his medications and that everything was in order. A doctor asked if it was possible Andrew could have taken extra Seroquel on his own. He asked me to go back home and check if all the Seroquel was where it belonged. I did, and there was none missing.

When I returned to St. Barnabas, I was informed that Andrew was in a coma. He would never emerge. A few days later, a neurologist informed me that Andrew was brain dead. I cut off life support two days later—in the same hospital complex where he was born fifteen and a half years earlier. Andrew's death was attributed to neuroleptic malignant syndrome, a rare but known side effect from prolonged high doses of atypical antipsychotic drugs, such as Seroquel.

CHAPTER THIRTEEN

Out of Deep Sadness, a New Commitment

October 13, 2013

If you haven't lost a child, it is impossible to know the deep crater of heartache that comes in its wake. Believing that I did everything I could to help Andrew is still worth nothing beside the fact that he died under my care.

How did I let it happen?

For three and half years, this question dominated my existence.

If you haven't lived it, you can't know the feeling of uncontrollable burning tears that pour out when the question pops into your head, apropos of nothing. Shortly after Andrew's death, I began seeing a psychiatrist, a psychologist, and a social worker for myself. The treatment I got was superb. Ironically, it came from the single-payer, nonprofit Veterans Administration health care system.[1] Contrary to what has been in the news, I had no problems getting appointments at the East Orange, New Jersey VA Hospital, sometimes three in one week. I was very lucky.

In April of 2010, I moved out of South Orange to the Jersey shore in order to avoid the painful, triggering reminders of my past family life: the schools, Flood Hill, South Orange Avenue, etc. I'd lost my wife, my son, my career trajectory, and my peace of mind—the main things I'd spent a life working toward. A year later I decided to return to consulting and write a new pharmaceutical market report. I needed both to re-establish my confidence and to make some money. It felt good to really dig back into my area of expertise. The work allowed me escape from my suffering as well.

During the winter I took frequent walks on the beach, having interior dialogues. I thought a lot about what my family had gone through, and how I could translate it into something beneficial for others. Andrew was gone. His spirit, his uncanny coordination and athleticism, and the pride and hope I felt for his future during his time at The Clarion School had vanished forever.

It took an enormous amount of time, suffering, and second-guessing of my motives to arrive at the decision to file a malpractice suit against Dr. Bainer. I knew that no possible outcome could bring back my son. It took all my emotional strength to ride the elevator up to the law office where Dr. Bainer waited with our respective lawyers for his deposition. My lawyer was a specialist in tort law, working on contingency. He represented clients seeking damages for wrongful injury. Dr. Bainer was represented by a defense specialist, contracted by his malpractice insurance provider.

From across the conference table, Dr. Bainer looked sloppy and disheveled. It's interesting how the same traits that I once read as wise and professorial, under the circumstances, sent a completely different signal. In my previous state of desperation for Andrew—for answers, for prescriptions, for anything that could help—perhaps my judgment was clouded. Seeing Dr. Bainer that morning brought a rush of feelings.

Some shocking information came to light in the deposition that left me even more apoplectic and sad. It turned out that Dr. Bainer had only practiced psychiatry for a few years when he began seeing Andrew. Despite the reassuringly calm and experienced demeanor that he presented, Dr. Bainer had actually spent most of his professional life as a lawyer. He was not even board-certified as a psychiatrist; he'd failed the psychiatry board exam twice. At the time I took him on, should I have been suspicious and checked him out more thoroughly? How could I have done that? Might a more experienced or qualified psychiatrist have recognized the side effect dangers for Andrew?

Through my personal research to make some sense of Andrew's death, I encountered disturbingly clear trends and conflicts of interest in the children's mental health care industry that placed my son, and ultimately my entire family, in unknown danger. My experience in the malpractice proceedings only helped solidify my feeling that I was fighting for something bigger than Andrew's memory. A new mission was beginning to take shape in my mind.

The cause of Andrew's fatal neuroleptic malignant syndrome was clear. His dose of Seroquel was 150% of the maximum FDA-approved dose for adults. Clinical research from 2008 showed no additional benefit for the drug in doses above 600 milligrams. Andrew had received 900 milligrams a day over six months, an excess of 54,000 milligrams into his approximately 120-pound fifteen-year-old body.

Still, Dr. Bainer and his insurance company came ready to battle. Dr. Bainer questioned the accuracy of the hospital's death certificate during the deposition. His lawyer later sought to demonstrate that death certificates are unreliable, even though Andrew's case was reviewed by multiple senior pathologists.

It's the professional prescriber's ultimate responsibility to convey a drug's risks. Dr. Bainer actually handwrote in Andrew's file that he "assumed" Andrew's school had enumerated Seroquel's dangers—the exact opposite of his steady refrain that the drug had "no side effects." I was shocked and tormented by the revelations in the deposition, imagining that each critical bit of information, provided before his death, might have saved Andrew.

I am amazed that Dr. Bainer was not legally required to make clear his weak professional status while managing Andrew's medication. To me, this non-disclosure was an ethical breach of the doctor-patient relationship. Furthermore, I believe it should be illegal for non-board-certified psychiatrists to prescribe to children without additional supervision. Had I known Dr. Bainer's actual professional status, I would have found someone else.

Dr. Bainer's style of practice is increasingly common in the children's mental health industry. There is a serious shortage of qualified prescribers in child psychiatry. With the explosion of reactive psychopharmacology pushed by parents, schools, and the marketplace, Dr. Bainer's business was simply following economic demand with the flexibility accorded a physician practicing off-label prescribing. More and more families are seeking help for their children in the form of diagnoses and prescriptions. They require licensed prescribing professionals. Today, many prescribers come from primary care, internal medicine, pediatrics, and other specialties. Whether properly trained or not, they are authorized to recommend drugs with impunity and without restriction.

The evolving marketplace—driven largely by the pharmaceutical companies and their elaborate marketing and lobbying, as well as the incentives of the for-profit insurance sector—is rife with financial and ethical conflicts of interest as well as, unfortunately, sloppy science. It's all too easy for the honorable and caring intentions of mental health professionals to be unconsciously swallowed up by these conflicts of interest, as well as consciously by baser financial motivations in our for-profit health care system.

Why did Dr. Bainer push the Seroquel so heavily? What could I have actually done to intervene? Dr. Bainer obviously didn't set out to hurt Andrew. With psychiatric drugs, though, results can be highly subjective and difficult to ascertain. The continuous, almost improvisational trial-and-error that I saw, often with highly potent drugs, is an alarmingly common practice. It's easy to imagine how the mechanisms of restraint can be gradually diluted and good judgment impacted. There is increased public and professional demand for pharmaceutical intervention. And the pressure on doctors' time and attention, largely driven by insurance providers' reimbursement schemes that reward the medication approach, only exacerbates the problem. The resulting dangers can be unfortunately severe.

From a medical expert opinion attached to our case:

Between March 2008 [and] July 2008, Andrew's dose of Seroquel was increased from approximately 400 mg per day to 900 mg a day. Unfortunately, Dr. Bainer cannot remember why this increase had occurred nor did he have any documentation that supported the reason for the increase. Furthermore, he had no documentation that this increase was discussed with Andrew's father. This admission constitutes gross negligence contrary to any known clinical practice medicating an adolescent with a potent drug, thereby increasing the need to monitor the reaction side effects, notify the parents and insure proper documentation. Dr. Bainer failed on all accounts. This failure is contrary to New Jersey standards of clinical practice and American Psychiatric Association standards of medical practice.

The official cause of death listed on Andrew's death certificate was neuroleptic malignant syndrome (NMS), a known side effect of high dosages of atypical antipsychotics. He showed multiple signs and symptoms of this condition—exactly what Dr. Bainer, practicing medication management for off-label drug use, should have been on the lookout for. There are mechanisms that can be used, such as a blood test to measure creatinase levels.[2]

How is it that our children can be given such potent drugs without even a basic foundation of scientific evidence to establish their safety or efficacy? Isn't that exactly what our regulatory bodies like the FDA are meant to provide?

The vast majority of these psychiatric medications have not been FDA-approved for use by children. As a result, the actual reason they are being prescribed to your child is not on the printed medication insert leaflet that lists the drug uses and other details, like you find on prescriptions for an allergy or an infection. The possible side effects are often buried in the long printouts and presented in legalese without clear prioritizing of frequency or severity. This is the reality of off-label prescribing practice.

I could not find any reliable statistics on deaths from NMS. It seems that either no one is collecting them, no one has expressed an interest, or the data is willfully obscured. I wonder how many cases like Andrew's are actually out there. I, for one, would like to know.

Our lawyer felt we had a strong case. An expert psychiatrist wrote the following opinion:

> Based upon the material evidence available in this case, it is my conclusion within a reasonable degree of medical and psychiatric certainty that Andrew Francesco suffered egregiously, physically and emotionally, from a classic case of neuroleptic malignant syndrome before and during his hospitalization. Similarly, his family suffered due to his missed diagnosis, medical crisis, psychiatric

mismanagement, and there are losses due to his premature death. It is also my conclusion, within a reasonable degree of medical and psychiatric certainty that, but for the grossly negligent assessment, diagnosis, physical treatment and coordination of care by Dr. Bainer, this young man would likely still be alive.

I'd hoped for significant compensation. It turned out, however, that the relevant legal precedent in New Jersey was a case from the 1970s (*Greene v. Bittner*) that largely negated compensation for the suffering and loss to me and Margaux. Compensation was instead tied to the estimated economic value of what Andrew would have given to me over my lifetime. For example, if he came to shovel my walk, that would be worth a bit of money. And, according to the precedent, I could have received a portion of Andrew's potential earnings—which, for a boy who died at fifteen while attending a special school, were estimated to be quite low. If he'd been a potential doctor, on the other hand, the financial compensation to me would have been greater. This is the absurdity of New Jersey malpractice tort law that I ran into. Thanks to this legal precedent, unknown to me at the time, it was difficult to even find a law firm that would take the case on contingency, since any settlement was expected to be relatively low.

According to a mediator that we were assigned early in the process, malpractice is almost always settled out of court and adheres to this forty-year-old New Jersey state legal precedent. When a malpractice case is settled out of court, of course, there is no requirement to enter the result into public record; hence the lack of available data, and one possible reason I couldn't find the incidence of deaths from NMS.

The net effect is a game that is rigged against the plaintiff, who has suffered the loss. The information on cause of death gets hidden, and the penalties for the prescriber are no more than a raise in next year's malpractice insurance.

The mediator further informed me that the few cases that end up in trial are almost always found in favor of the doctor. He put out tremendous pressure to settle for the sum of $175,000 immediately. "That's what it is worth," he said, emotionlessly. He claimed there was data to support this number. The mediator, though, had two strong incentives to press for a settlement: Firstly, he would be compensated for a successful mediation. Secondly, successful mediations might recommend him for more and bigger mediation cases and, ultimately, bigger success fees for him.

The malpractice defense team naturally wanted to settle at a low price and keep cases off the public record. They also had a strong and recurring need to press for this kind of mediation. Of course, they performed this exercise multiple times per year and were experts on the subject.

I eventually decided to accept an offer of $225,000, made through my lawyer and not the mediator. In December of 2013, I received a check. After the expenses and the contingency commission, I netted about $100,000: a shockingly low dollar value in exchange for my son's life.

However, the process was extremely educational. Though it was upsetting to relive painful experiences and to detail the numerous examples of Andrew's mistreatment, I was able to re-examine many events and influences throughout the ordeal from a clear distance and on the basis of facts. As a caregiving parent, I often felt in the dark. I can now see many decisions and conditions much better, as well as mistakes that could have been avoided. It is my main reason for writing this book.

It's clear that the "invisible hand" of the market has pushed the toxic children's mental health industry toward a single-minded medication-only approach, with drugs that are largely ineffective and have horrible side effects. The invisible hand has caused pandemic overmedication and a corresponding gross undertreatment by squelching alternative therapies. There is a large and growing body of literature on the ineffectiveness and dangers of psychiatric drugs for children, written by great journalists, concerned mental health professionals, and researchers. Quite tragically, families are experiencing far fewer therapeutic alternatives to medication, and more coercion from schools to medicate. Many "old-school" doctors are even being pressured by the insurance companies to reduce therapy or perform it without reimbursement, meaning that parents must pay out-of-pocket. This leaves a huge segment of the population without this option: the option that did the most to help Andrew.

Meanwhile, the drug and insurance industries are profiting at amazing levels, as are some doctors. There needs to be a pushback. From my professional life, I know the health care industry better than most, and I have now also played the unfortunate role of a confused and exploited consumer. What has helped me most to overcome the grief of losing my son is the compulsion to share what I have learned and to use my expertise and energy to create change. It is time to organize and enact practical reforms toward reversing the trends and conflicts that inflict harm on millions of innocent children and families.

I hope you will join me. If interested, kindly read the following Afterword.

AFTERWORD

January 2015

This book has been a long and sometimes difficult exercise. It has been cathartic for me, extremely interesting to research and write, and hopefully useful and valuable for you. As a father, I felt compelled to bring the material to your attention. I loved my son and miss him every day. I felt that I did everything in my power to help him overcome his mental health condition, but our children's mental health care system has evolved to vex children and parents in what is often their most confused and susceptible state of mind.

As should be apparent by now, I firmly believe we have a serious systemic problem within the children's mental health industry. I am not a doctor blamer, a pharmaceutical/insurance industry basher, or a school system critic. On the contrary, I support most of their collective activities. We do not live in a perfect world.

However, from time to time every industry needs to go through a period of reform. Now is the time to shake up this industry that has become toxic to many of its innocent patients. Reform is entirely possible. It has happened, in part, in other industries (sectors in banking, Wall Street insider trading, chemical pollution, ecology, etc.). Every effort of this nature seems naïve in the beginning. The challenge seems so daunting, and the forces resistant to change so entrenched. However, I feel it is worth the effort to give it a try.

It will take funds and the building of a strong team to begin to tackle what I believe are solvable problems that stem from the many major deficiencies in today's toxic children's mental health industry. The futures of literally millions of children can be positively impacted by the right efforts by the right people.

Andrew was a lively, funny, and caring child. He had a great sense of humor and incredible coordination. Although he struggled with mental health problems—as well as frequent, destabilizing school reassignments—for most of his young life, I thought he was finally getting better and on the road to becoming a truly happy person. His doctors and pharmacists never once indicated the possibility of such dangerous side effects as NMS from the drugs he was prescribed. Now he's gone forever. Will your children become the next victims? Or your grandchildren?

I still ask myself, how could I have let this happen? Could I have done anything differently? Should I have done more research around his condition and his treatment protocol? Could I have asked more questions of his doctors? I've asked myself these questions hundreds of times. Like most parents with a child in crisis, however, I relied mainly on the expertise and advice of medical professionals. I didn't suspect that despite the good intentions of his doctors, larger trends put my son in jeopardy and would ultimately kill him.

For the last twenty-one years, I've been an independent pharmaceutical and healthcare consultant. Among other things, I advise pharmaceutical companies on how to most profitably navigate market shifts as drugs move off patent. I am not a doctor or a mental health professional, but through my thirty years of work in the health care industry, as well as my experience with Andrew, I've gained unusually deep, 360-degree, all-dimensional knowledge of the children's mental health industry in this country. Even as a well-paid health care expert, though, I'm a relatively small cog within a large and byzantine industry. Up until Andrew's sudden death, my knowledge of children's mental health care came mostly from my experiences with his treatment. I was unaware of the serious issue of inappropriate and systematized overprescribing of powerful drugs to children—drugs that in most cases were designed and approved for adults only. I was unaware of alternative approaches that could have mitigated or even eliminated the stressed need for drugs. I was unaware of the insidious influence of the profit motive in all aspects of treatment.

After two years of painful mourning, self-reproach, and self-imposed isolation, I slowly began to push through my grief with the help of therapists and friends. I began to look for an explanation of how my son could lose his life in less than thirty-six hours by taking a prescribed dose of Seroquel under the care of medical professionals.

As I began research, I discovered some appalling trends and practices—often basic and unfortunately common profit-driven industry characteristics—that end up counteracting the essential goals of health care. I discovered dispiriting, system-wide problems in mental health care that put millions of children at risk every day in this country. The entire industry is begging for reform. This is a systemic problem. There's lots to do.

Below, I've listed five major areas of concern.

1. Overmedicating Our Children, with Special Focus on the Atypical Antipsychotic Drugs: There is no greater example of the systemic flaws in our current toxic children's mental health industry than in the area of drugging our children. Unfortunately, children currently receiving psychiatric treatment are likely to be the most exposed and "at-risk" population segment in the United States. The lack of safeguards is astonishing, given the size of the potential medicated child population segment (58 million aged four through seventeen) and the $45 billion of psychiatric medication prescribed to them annually. The chart below details the safeguards for adults taking psychotropic medication versus children.

Psychotropic Medication Use Safeguards
Adult vs. Child

SAFEGUARD	ADULT	CHILD
Labeling **Purpose:** Providing use and safety instructions, usually in the package insert leaflet **Responsibility:** Drug companies, FDA	Yes, always.	More than 80% of "off-label" psychotropic prescribing has no relevant instructions approved by the FDA. More broadly, entire classes of drugs have no FDA-reviewed pediatric data.
"Best Practices" **Purpose:** Generally accepted guidelines for prescribing physicians **Responsibility:** Prescribers	Yes, always.	Very little to none. No consistent quality information on dosing, polypharmacy, drug interactions. Sloppy record-keeping.

SAFEGUARD	ADULT	CHILD
Drug Safety Software **Purpose:** Covers proper dosing, interactions, etc. **Responsibility:** Retail pharmacist	Yes, always.	None. The absence of hard data is the excuse software is not available. However, broad guidelines could be adopted, such as from HEDIS (see Notes, Afterword, #6).
Large-Scale Physician Practice Monitoring and Policy Creation **Purpose:** Generation of safety, efficacy, and cost data **Responsibility:** Insurance companies	Yes, often and increasing in frequency; largely driven by their interest in lowering costs.	Best outcomes for children are not the goals. Instead, concerns are quarterly profit and reliable cash flow and financial forecasting. Programs with successful outcomes that go beyond one year rejected in favor of long-term generic drug use.

Imagine it. A $45 billion drug market, largely unregulated, barely monitored, and with few controls. Our children have scant protection. Pharmacists have software to adjust and advise adult patients, but there is none for children. Off-label prescribing is 80% of that $45 million and strictly up to the commitment of individual doctors to diagnose, prescribe, and monitor the child. This lack of regulatory structure, absence of reliable data, and high dependence on the doctor's judgment is obscene. Moreover, there are many complex decisions for the parents with little information to guide them and scant time in the day to search for answers. All of these and other flaws in the system are what killed my son.

I am particularly worried about the continued expansion of atypical antipsychotic drugs. As recently as twenty years ago, first-generation antipsychotic drugs, such as Haldol, were rarely prescribed to either adults or children because they were widely known to carry a high risk of serious side effects. Around 1992, however, a new class of antipsychotics came onto the market. They were reported to have fewer side effects and became known as second-generation "atypical" antipsychotic drugs. This highly potent class of drugs includes Johnson & Johnson's Risperdal, known generically as risperidone; Eli Lilly's Zyprexa or olanzapine; Bristol-Myers Squibb and Otsuka Pharmaceutical's Abilify or aripiprazole; and AstraZeneca's Seroquel or quetiapine. There are others.

Today, atypical antipsychotic drug sales are about $16 billion annually, and they are second in sales as a prescription drug class only to oncology drugs. More concerning to me is that this class of drug has exploded in use and become the one most commonly prescribed in the U.S. to children.[1]

According to this 2012 study, since 1993 the rate of antipsychotic drug prescriptions to U.S. children overall has increased 600%, and antipsychotic prescriptions to teens have quintupled. Virtually all of this growth is from prescriptions for second-generation atypical antipsychotics.

Despite the alleged safety increases over the first-generation medications, these drugs are not harmless. They can cause diabetes and weight gain, among a host of other serious side effects. Additionally, they cost far more than the older medications. Doctors routinely prescribe these powerful drugs for a wide range of conditions or disruptive behavior disorders in children: everything from anger, aggression, and severe mood swings, to bipolar disorder, to Asperger's syndrome and autism. Are too many kids taking antipsychotic drugs? Yes! *Consumer Reports* completed an excellent 2013 report (financed by drug company penalty payments, by the way) that shows the terrible threat to our children and offers excellent advice.[2]

When Andrew died, there was no FDA-approved clinical evidence that these drugs were suitable for children, or indicating what dosage was appropriate over what period of time. Today the FDA has approved a few uses for children, but the evidence is limited to a relatively small number of short-term studies.[3] It's still unclear how well the drugs actually work and whether they remain effective over the long term. Cumulatively, studies of these drugs have involved fewer than 3,000 children, most of them followed for eight weeks or less. The pharmacy benefit manager company Medco (now part of Express Scripts, with a database of millions of patients) specifically asserts that atypical antipsychotics have been overused and carry potentially very serious long-term side effects such as diabetes and other metabolic diseases.[4]

2. Drug Distribution Systems: Without FDA guidelines, medical professionals are able to prescribe antipsychotic drugs to children using their own judgment under the practice known as "off-label" prescribing. The practice allows doctors to prescribe drugs for conditions or to populations for which they are not specifically approved, as long as the doctors practice "medication management." In effect, each individual doctor must try to customize the drugs prescribed to the child in the absence of meaningful scientific data regarding dosage size or lingering effects. The weight of this task should not be underestimated, given the strength of the medications and the increasing time pressures on most doctors today.

An additional danger to our children is the fact that medical professionals neither specializing in psychiatry nor trained in prescribing these drugs—pediatricians and internal medicine/general practitioners—are prescribing them at increasing rates.[5] Millions of children are put at risk each year by this relatively haphazard and uncharted practice. There has simply been no sufficient clinical study or traditional FDA approval process tracking the effects of these powerful drugs on developing brains and bodies.

One might assume, given the huge segment of the underage population in question and the billions of dollars spent on these medications for children, that the FDA would pursue and institute regulations regarding their use. One might assume a sufficient demand for more scientific evidence from clinical testing of these drugs for children. Strangely, there remains very little public data. Standardized best practice efforts for prescribing (HEDIS) are being developed by the psychiatric industry for announcement in 2015,[6] but these efforts have no enforcement power, are woefully incomplete, and are unlikely to be followed in a timely fashion.

What remains a grave concern for me is the diagnostic flexibility of the prescribers. That they don't know exactly what is going on appears to be an increasingly difficult argument to accept. A growing body of literature supports the idea that there is absolutely no evidence, whether clinical or empirical, to justify the use of most of these off-label drugs in children to correct a chemical deficiency. In most cases the drugs are, at minimum, intended to slow children down physically, mask symptoms, and create the illusion that something positive may be going on. More and more evidence points to neurological issues as the actual root of many problems. In other words, the problem is with the "circuitry" of the brain and not a chemical imbalance. More needs to be learned. Prescribing these drugs is hitting something completely different, which, as in my son's case, can ultimately be pointless and lethal.

3. Illegal Drug Promotion: Pharmaceutical companies have been a major contributor to the problem of overmedication. Between 2009 and 2014, drug makers were fined in excess of $12 billion[7] for abusive trade practices that involved, in large part, illegally encouraging the prescription of antipsychotic drugs for non-FDA-approved uses, such as treatment of children. There continue to be numerous lawsuits filed by families of children who suffered serious side effects from these drugs. Yet the practice appears to continue in force, too often pushing past an already distressingly wide legal gray area.

Pharmaceutical companies pursue regulatory requirements from the FDA by engaging in expensive clinical testing, often investing tens of millions of dollars in the research and development of a new prescription drug. Once approved by the FDA, the drug becomes part of the tool kit used by medical professionals to treat conditions. Pharmaceutical companies have found that they can extend their market significantly by encouraging off-label uses. Though promotion of off-label uses is illegal, the enormous fines on record indicate the breadth and intensity of this practice by drug companies.

4. Insurance Company Incentives for Drugs: Big pharma is only one piece in this dangerous, profit-driven game, in which incentives are often misaligned with successful treatment of our children. A study[8] shows that there has been a substantial increase in psychiatrists who focus their practices on medication management, devoting less time to non-pharmaceutical treatments like traditional talk therapy. Specifically, the study showed that between 1996 and 2005, in conjunction with the introduction of second-generation atypical antipsychotics, psychotherapy visits declined 35%. More compelling, perhaps, is the fact that the overall number of psychiatrists who even offered psychotherapy as an option to their patients declined by a stunning 43%. According to the report, these declines coincided with changes in reimbursement for psychotherapy and increased incentives for medication management.

For the psychiatrists, it seems that there was a gradual push toward a new business model. The traditional session time for talk therapy was fifty minutes, for which the psychiatrist would be compensated at least $150–$200 (in 2002 dollars, when this study was done). In that same period of time, a psychiatrist could see three medication management patients, and potentially double his or her hourly revenue.[9] Psychiatrists began to change the focus of their efforts. That trend has continued today.[10]

The insurance companies encourage this medication management approach over talk therapy via their reimbursement schemes, since it is easier to forecast and quantify. Also, in an effort to fulfill their quarterly financial obligations to their shareholders, insurance companies are seeking to satisfy two objectives: one, to keep payments to doctors as low as possible; two, to keep financial forecasts as predictable as possible by normalizing routine twenty-minute medication management sessions. This is preferable to paying the doctors for ongoing talk therapy sessions, which often also run concurrently with medications. The insurance companies' incentive is, of course, also to reduce the number of sessions that individual patients spend with psychiatrists. Psychiatrists bill at a higher rate than non-M.D. therapists for talk therapy. To make more money under this incentive system, the psychiatrists are encouraged to see more patients without the more labor-intensive involvement that is necessary for talk therapy. Easily lost in the shuffle here is the original purpose: to treat patients as effectively as possible and improve the health care outcome.

The financial incentives for the primary players in the children's mental health industry have devalued the individual patient. That needs to change.

5. Information for Patients and Their Families on the Children's Mental Health Industry: From deep personal experience,

I know how hard it is to find reliable information relevant to choosing doctors, schools, and therapies. For example, how do you know if a certain prescriber falls into the 20% of practitioners that typically prescribe 80% of the overall drugs within a particular therapy area? The drug companies certainly have this information. What tactics, questions, and databases can help families find practitioners who agree that children are overmedicated and undertreated?

The children's mental health industry needs to be recognized for what it is and challenged. The practice of off-label prescribing, inadequate medication management, a lack of research into the long-term effects of atypical antipsychotic drugs on children, and inadequate and poorly designed family and patient resources all contributed to my son's untimely death.

In telling the story of Andrew's battle against his mental health problems and our family's frustrating and confusing experience maneuvering through the fractured system of mental health care on his behalf, I hope this book will serve not only as a testament to his memory, but also as a cautionary tale to the millions of other children and families faced with similar conditions. After nearly twenty years of increasingly common practice, the prescription of atypical antipsychotic drugs, to my astonishment, remains largely unregulated and unsafe for our innocent children.

Until the multi-billion-dollar children's mental health industry is forced to shift focus to the patient, to change its profit-driven practices of dangerous, ill-managed overmedication and undertreatment, the health and well-being of all our vulnerable children remain in jeopardy. While there are some positive initiatives being pursued toward improving outcomes, the overall effort is still well below what we need for true reform.

We deserve better. I know my son Andrew deserved better.

We have a profound and growing problem with today's toxic children's mental health industry and its systemic flaws.

I've chosen to do something about it. I invite you to please join me. If you'd like to help pursue a solution with me, please read the following section, in which I provide a brief overview of what I feel is needed for true and meaningful reform. I welcome your feedback at my personal website, stevenfrancesco.com, or the website for this book, OvermedicatedandUndertreated.com.

Sincerely

Steven Francesco
New York City
July 2015

Introducing DoNoHarmNetwork.Org

T here is a terrific need to improve health outcomes for children and provide more hope to struggling parents and families. In the absence of the realistic possibility of moving to a single-payer health care system in our lifetime, there is a need to identify areas where significant modification can make a difference in a reasonable amount of time.

Below are some primary areas of concern with correspondingly recommended broad solutions:

Paradigm Shifts Needed

CONCERN	SOLUTION
Medical & Pharmaceutical Orientation	Holistic Support
Professionals in Their Own Worlds/Silos	Collaborative Care
Physician-Dominated	Patient/Consumer Focus
Reactive	Proactive
Fragmented Care	Integrated Care
Pay-per-Episode	Pay for Continuum Care Leading to Better Outcomes
School Alternatives Chaotic	Consistent, High-Standard Alternative Schools

Introducing DoNoHarmNetwork.Org. Each of the above points needs to be expanded with action steps. I have made a beginning on this new website. But I can't do this alone. A team must be built, financing found, and a network put together.

I have a business plan that addresses some of the above. I look forward to learning your area and level of interest. Please visit DoNoHarmNetwork.Org so we can start working together to expand our knowledge and usefulness and, ultimately, have a positive impact on today's toxic children's mental health industry and reverse the medication epidemic. Thank you.

Notes

The Notes section is designed to help readers gain a deeper understanding of particular issues mentioned in the book. Generally, I have provided information that was current at the time of the event and that may have guided me, as well as more recent information to further assist those who may need it. There is far more information on the book website, Overmedicatedand-Undertreated.com com as well as DoNoHarmNetwork.Org.

Introduction

1. Benzer T. Neuroleptic malignant syndrome. *Medscape.* http://emedicine.medscape.com/article/816018-overview

   Neuroleptic malignant syndrome (NMS) is a rare, but life-threatening, idiosyncratic reaction to neuroleptic medications that is characterized by fever, muscular rigidity, altered mental status, and autonomic dysfunction. NMS often occurs shortly after the initiation of neuroleptic treatment, or after dose increases. Signs and symptoms: The key to diagnosis is that NMS occurs only after exposure to an neuroleptic drug. On average, onset is 4-14 days after the start of therapy; 90% of cases occur within 10 days. **However, NMS can occur years into therapy. Once the syndrome starts, it usually evolves over 24-72 hours.**

Chapter One: The Beginning

1. Absence seizures. *Epilepsy Foundation.* http://www.epilepsy.com/learn/types-seizures/absence-seizures

"Absence seizures: An absence seizure causes a short period of 'blanking out' or staring into space. Like other kinds of seizures, they are caused by abnormal activity in a person's brain. You may also hear people call absence seizures petit mal seizures, although that name is not common anymore. There are two types of absence seizures:

- *Simple absence seizures:* During a simple absence seizure, a person usually just stares into space for less than 10 seconds. Because they happen so quickly, it's very easy not to notice simple absence seizures — or to confuse them with daydreaming or not paying attention.
- *Complex absence seizures:* During a complex absence seizure, a person will make some kind of movement in addition to staring into space. Movements may include blinking, chewing, or hand gestures. A complex absence seizure can last up to 20 seconds."

Chapter Two: Different Sides Emerge

1. Vitiello B. Pharmacotherapy of the Preschool ADHD Treatment Study (PATS) children growing up. *J Am Acad Child Adolesc Psychiatry.* 2015;54(7):550–556.

"About 65% of preschool children who were diagnosed with ADHD and given stimulant drugs were still taking those drugs three and six years later. About 10% were also being prescribed an antipsychotic."

Chapter Three: The FDA Meeting

1. As part of my consulting business, we launched a global newsletter, entitled SWITCH.

My presentation was preceded by this article: http://www.fda.gov/ohrms/dockets/ac/01/public%20hearing/3737op_17_francesco.htm

Chapter Four: Flood Hill, Carving a New Path

1. Ali S, Ajmal S. When is off-label prescribing appropriate? *Current Psychiatry*. 2012;11(7). http://www.currentpsychiatry.com/index.php?id=22661&tx_ttnews%5Btt_news%5D=176928

"Off-label prescribing often is not supported by strong evidence and carries clinical risks, such as adverse effects and unproven efficacy. A 2006 study found that only 4% of off-label prescriptions of psychiatric medications were supported by strong scientific evidence."

2. Gaudiano B. Psychotherapy's image problem. *New York Times*. September 29, 2013. http://www.nytimes.com/2013/09/30/opinion/psychotherapys-image-problem.html

"Psychotherapy is in decline. In the United States, from 1998 to 2007, the number of patients in outpatient mental health facilities receiving psychotherapy alone fell by 34 percent, while the number receiving medication alone increased by 23 percent."

3. Brooks D. Heroes of uncertainty. *New York Times*. May 27, 2013. http://www.nytimes.com/2013/05/28/opinion/brooks-heroes-of-uncertainty.html

"Psychiatrists use terms like 'mental disorder' and 'normal behavior,' but there is no agreement on what these concepts mean. When you look at the definitions psychiatrists habitually use to define various ailments, you see that they contain vague words that wouldn't pass muster in any actual scientific analysis: 'excessive,' 'binge,' 'anxious.'"

Chapter Five: On the Beach at Rockport

1. In 2003, the body of literature, both positive and negative, surrounding the safety and efficacy of the second-generation atypical antipsychotic drugs was just emerging. Fortunately, there are numerous articles now available on the problems with the atypical antipsychotic drugs. There are many references in these Notes. A more extensive list is at OvermedicatedandUndertreated.com. Also, a good current summary is at http://www.webmd.com/mental-health/news/20110107/study-newer-antipsychotic-drugs-are-overused.

2. Ego depletion. *Wikipedia*. https://en.wikipedia.org/wiki/Ego_depletion

    "Ego depletion refers to the idea that self-control and other mental processes that require focused conscious effort rely on energy that can be used up. When that energy is low (rather than high), mental activity that requires self-control is impaired. In other words, using one's self-control impairs the ability to control one's self later on. In this sense, the idea of (limited) willpower is correct."

3. The Adam Lanza / Newtown, Connecticut tragedy in December 2012 comes to mind. This is not to say that Andrew could have become seriously violent; however, many parents do experience genuine fear of their children. For a useful discussion, see: Solomon A. The reckoning: The father of the Sandy Hook Killer searches for answers. *The New Yorker*. March 17, 2014. Also see the Letters section response to this article two weeks later.

Chapter Six: Turning Outside the District for Relief

1. Wertheimer A. Off-label but on point? *Pharmaceutical Executive.* April 1, 2011. http://www.pharmexec.com/label-point?rel=canonical

"Something is definitely wrong if nearly 50 percent of all prescriptions written in the US are 'off-label.' Are physicians becoming reckless; is the FDA having trouble keeping pace; are patients making unrealistic demands on the health system, or is it all of the above? ... Perhaps the largest area of off-label use is in pediatrics."

2. Zito J. A three-country comparison of psychotropic medication prevalence in youth. *Child Adolesc Psychiatry Ment Health.* 2008;2:26. http://www.capmh.com/content/2/1/26

Good but old data. Needs to be updated, and the U.S. situation is likely to be far worse now.

"The annual prevalence of any psychotropic medication in youth was significantly greater in the US (6.7%) than in the Netherlands (2.9%) and in Germany (2.0%). Antidepressant and stimulant prevalence were 3 or more times greater in the US than in the Netherlands and Germany, while antipsychotic prevalence was 1.5–2.2 times greater. The atypical antipsychotic subclass represented only 5% of antipsychotic use in Germany, but 48% in the Netherlands and 66% in the US."

Chapter Seven: Lightning Strikes

1. Kowalski JM. Medication-induced dystonic reactions. *Medscape.* http://emedicine.medscape.com/article/814632-overview

"Dystonic drug reactions are reversible extrapyramidal effects that can occur after administration of a neuroleptic drug. Symptoms may begin immediately or can be delayed hours to days. Although a wide variety of medications can elicit symptoms, the typical antipsychotics are most often responsible. Dystonic reactions (ie, dyskinesias) are characterized by intermittent spasmodic or sustained involuntary contractions of muscles in the face, neck, trunk, pelvis, extremities, and even the larynx. Although dystonic reactions are rarely life threatening, the adverse effects often cause distress for patients and families."

2. Buyer's Remorse Video: http://www.youtube.com/watch? v=xvaPF_y-fiU

Chapter Eight: Then Thunder

1. Stroke. *Mayo Clinic*. http://www.mayoclinic.org/diseases-conditions/stroke/symptoms-causes/dxc-20117265

"A stroke occurs when the blood supply to your brain is interrupted or reduced. This deprives your brain of oxygen and nutrients, which can cause your brain cells to die. A stroke may be caused by a blocked artery (ischemic stroke) or the leaking or bursting of a blood vessel (hemorrhagic stroke). Some people may experience only a temporary disruption of blood flow to their brain (transient ischemic attack, or TIA)."

Chapter Nine: Only Hope Remains

1. Natal teeth. *MedlinePlus*. http://www.nlm.nih.gov/medlin-eplus/ency/article/003268.htm

"Natal teeth are teeth that are already present at the time of birth. They are different from neonatal teeth, which grow in during the first 30 days after birth. Natal teeth are uncommon. They are present in about 1 in every 2,000 to 3,000 births. Natal teeth most often develop on the lower gum, where the central incisor teeth will appear. They have little root structure. They are attached to the end of the gum by soft tissue and are often wobbly. Natal teeth are usually not well-formed, but they may cause irritation and injury to the infant's tongue when nursing. Natal teeth may also be uncomfortable for a nursing mother. Natal teeth are often removed shortly after birth while the newborn infant is still in the hospital."

Chapter Ten: Back on the Beach at Rockport

1. Goliszek A. How stress affects the immune system. *Psychology Today Blog*. November 12, 2014. https://www.psychologytoday.com/blog/how-the-mind-heals-the-body/201411/how-stress-affects-the-immune-system

"Ongoing stress makes us susceptible to illness and disease because the brain sends defense signals to the endocrine system, which then releases an array of hormones that not only gets us ready for emergency situations but severely depresses our immunity at the same time. Some experts claim that stress is responsible for as much as 90% of all illnesses and diseases, including cancer and heart disease. The way it does this is by triggering chemical reactions and flooding the body with cortisol that, among other things, decreases inflammation, decreases white blood cells and NK cells (special cells that kill cancer), increases tumor development and growth, and increases the rate of infection and tissue damage."

Chapter Eleven: Redemption

1. Animal-assisted therapy. *Wikipedia*. https://en.wikipedia.org/wiki/Animal-assisted_therapy

"Animal-assisted therapy (AAT) is a type of therapy that involves animals as a form of treatment. The goal of AAT is to improve a patient's social, emotional, or cognitive functioning. Advocates state that animals can be useful for educational and motivational effectiveness for participants. A therapist who brings along a pet may be viewed as being less threatening, increasing the rapport between patient and therapist. Wilson's (1984) biophilia hypothesis is based on the premise that our attachment to and interest in animals stems from the strong possibility that human survival was partly dependent on signals from animals in the environment indicating safety or threat. The biophilia hypothesis suggests that now, if we see animals at rest or in a peaceful state, this may signal to us safety, security and feelings of well-being which in turn may trigger a state where personal change and healing are possible."

Chapter Twelve: Interrupted

1. This pediatrician clearly understood and executed "best practices" in all he did. For example, when we asked him to prescribe Ritalin after we decided that the child psychiatrist was unbearably arrogant, he eventually told us that he was not trained in this area and told us to find someone else. He clearly understood his role and his professional limits.

Chapter Thirteen: Out of Deep Sadness, a New Commitment

1. I served three years in the U.S. Army after high school and before entering Columbia University in 1970. Included was a tour of duty in the Mekong Delta of Vietnam as a medic.

2. Benzer T. Neuroleptic malignant syndrome. *Medscape.* http://emedicine.medscape.com/article/816018-overview

"Diagnosis: No laboratory test result is diagnostic for NMS. Laboratory studies are used to assess severity and complications or rule out other diagnostic possibilities. A summary of the laboratory abnormalities that may be found in neuroleptic malignant syndrome includes the following: Increased LDH, Increased creatine kinase (50-100% of cases), Increased AST and ALT, Increased alkaline phosphatase, Hyperuricemia."

Afterword

1. Olfson M, Blanco C, Liu S, Wang S, Correll C. National trends in the office-based treatment of children, adolescents, and adults with antipsychotics. *Arch Gen Psychiatry.* 2012;69(12):1247-1256. http://archpsyc.jamanetwork.com/article.aspx?articleid=1263977

"Results: Between 1993-1998 and 2005-2009, visits that resulted in a prescription of atypical antipsychotic medication increased

- for children, more than seven times more;
- for adolescents, almost five times more;
- for youths overall more than six times more;"

2. Are too many kids taking antipsychotic drugs? *Consumer Reports.* December 2013. http://www.consumerreports. org/cro/2013/12/are-too-many-kids-taking-antipsychotic-drugs/index.htm

An excellent, readable report that should be mandatory reading when the first atypical antipsychotic prescription is written. To quote the opening paragraph: "The number of children taking powerful antipsychotic drugs has nearly tripled over the last 10 to 15 years, according to recent research. The increase comes not because of an epidemic of schizophrenia or other forms of serious mental illness in children, but because doctors are increasingly prescribing the drugs to treat behavior problems, a use not approved by the Food and Drug Administration (FDA). And a disproportionate number of those prescriptions are written for poor and minority children, some as young as age 2."

3. Cohen D, Bonnot O, Bodeau N et al. Adverse effects of second-generation antipsychotics in children and adolescents: a Bayesian meta-analysis. *J Clin Psychopharmacol.* 2012;32:309-16. http://www.ncbi.nlm.nih.gov/pubmed/22544019

"We conclude that short-term metabolic effects and EPS (extrapyramidal syndrome) are frequent in children treated with SGAs (Second Generation Antipsychotics). Second-generation antipsychotics have distinct profiles of secondary effects, which should be considered in making treatment decisions."

4. Medco. America's state of mind report. *WHO Essential Medicines and Health Products Information Portal.* http://apps.who.int/medicinedocs/en/d/Js19032en/

"Increased use of atypical antipsychotics, especially among children may be due to the fact that they are seen as less dangerous than older antipsychotics and can be helpful for conditions that were previously treated with other medications. However, these drugs are not without their risks. There is evidence that the risk of diabetes and metabolic disorders from using atypical antipsychotics could be much more severe for pediatric patients than adults, and there is a need for more studies to understand the long-term effects of these drugs on children. Some of these drugs have warning labels regarding the possible exacerbation or increased risk of new-onset diabetes, although the metabolic side effects appear to be somewhat different for each drug."

5. Olfson M, Blanco C, Wang S, Laje G, Correll C. National trends in the mental health care of children, adolescents, and adults by office-based physicians. *JAMA Psychiatry.* 2014;71(1):81-90. http://archpsyc.jamanetwork.com/article.aspx?articleid=1784344

"Compared with adult mental health care, the mental health care of young people has increased more rapidly and has coincided with increased psychotropic medication use. A great majority of mental health care in office-based medical practice to children, adolescents, and adults is provided by non-psychiatrist physicians calling for increased consultation and communication between specialties."

6. The Healthcare Effectiveness Data and Information Set (HEDIS) is a tool used by more than 90% of America's health plans to measure performance on important dimensions of care and service. http://www.ncqa.org/HEDISQualityMeasurement.aspx.

7. Groeger L. Big Pharma's Big Fines. *ProPublica.* February 24, 2014. http://projects.propublica.org/graphics/bigpharma

An excellent summary with superb detail. Most of the financial penalty was from the illegal promotion of atypical antipsychotics to children.

"In the last few years pharmaceutical companies have agreed to pay over $13 billion to resolve U.S. Department of Justice allegations of fraudulent marketing practices, including the promotion of medicines for uses that were not approved by the Food and Drug Administration."

8. Olfson M, Marcus S. National trends in outpatient psycho-therapy. *Am J Psychiatry.* 2010;167:12. http://www.ncbi.nlm.nih.gov/pubmed/20686187.

A sea change in the profile of psychiatry as a profession.

"CONCLUSIONS: During the decade from 1998 to 2007, the percentage of the general population who used psychotherapy remained stable. Over the same period, however, psychotherapy assumed a less prominent role in outpatient mental health care as a large and increasing proportion of mental health outpatients received psychotropic medication without psychotherapy."

9. West J, Wilk J, Rae D, Narrow W, Regier D. Financial dis-incentives for the provision of psychotherapy. *Psych Serv.* 2003;54(12):1582. http://ps.psychiatryonline.org

10. Harris G. Talk doesn't pay so psychiatry turns instead to drug therapy, *New York Times.* March 5, 2011. http://www.ny-times.com/2011/03/06/health/policy/06doctors.html

"Like many of the nation's 48,000 psychiatrists, Dr. Levin, in large part because of changes in how much insurance will pay, no longer provides talk therapy, the form of psychiatry popularized by Sigmund Freud that dominated the profession for decades. In-stead, he prescribes medication, usually after a brief consultation with each patient. So Dr. Levin sent the man away with a referral to a less costly therapist and a personal crisis unexplored and un-resolved."

Acknowledgements

Overmedicated and Undertreated was a four-year effort that required significant discussion with and support from others. It is impossible to thank everyone who has been involved. The following names are simply a few of the many who contributed

For reading drafts and valuable feedback, I want to thank Elizabeth Rosenthal, Senior Writer, *New York Times* and Dr. Mark Olfson, Professor of Psychiatry, Columbia University Medical Center, Frank Ferrise, Ph.D. and Doris Peter, Ph.D. of *Consumer Reports*. Also, Mrs. Donna Toulouse, Ms. Naomi Decter, Mrs. Martha Bullen.

I want to thank William "Jake" Cosden for his valuable copyediting assistance and collaborative spirit.

Finally, I want to thank the numerous other authors and colleagues who have contributed large amounts of research and analysis on the serious distortions that have occurred in mental health in this country over the last 35 years. Their work, as well as active discussion by them and others, will be listed and enlivened on my book's website, OvermedicatedandUndertreated.com as well as DoNoHarmNetwork.com..

About the Author

MR. STEVEN FRANCESCO is uniquely quali-
fied to analyze, write about, and rec-
ommend reforms for the current
children's mental health industry. He
has over thirty years of experience in
today's health care industry and deep
functional knowledge of all sectors.
For the past four years, triggered by the tragic and sudden death
of his son, Andrew, Mr. Francesco has dedicated his consider-
able experience and skills to seeking ways to prevent this type of
lethal event from happening to other families.

He is the president and founder of Francesco International
LLC (www.franint.com), a twenty-one-year-old health care consultancy with a focus on converting prescription drugs to over-
the-counter status. He worked for pharmaceutical companies in
senior management for nine years.

Mr. Francesco is a highly respected and active thought leader.
He has testified five times publicly before the U.S. Food and Drug
Administration (FDA) on a broad range of policy issues, in addition to running numerous meetings on confidential product-
related issues.

In addition, Mr. Francesco has authored over fifty articles and
essays regarding the pharmaceutical industry. He is a recognized
expert on product life cycle issues. Mr. Francesco has been an invited speaker in the U.S., U.K., France, Germany, Australia, Israel,
Turkey, and Canada, and a frequently interviewed expert for national television and print media.

Mr. Francesco graduated with honors from Columbia University, where he earned his B.A. and M.B.A. He also earned Vietnam Service and Campaign ribbons after serving a tour of duty in the U.S. Army as a medic in the Mekong Delta of Vietnam. Mr. Francesco speaks fluent French and passing German. He resides in New York City.

ANDREW FRANCESCO
1993–2009

Made in the USA
Lexington, KY
10 June 2016